THE

Biblical
Greek

COMPANION

FOR BIBLE SOFTWARE USERS

GRAMMATICAL TERMS
EXPLAINED FOR EXEGESIS

Mark L. Strauss

ZONDERVAN®

ZONDERVAN

The Biblical Greek Companion for Bible Software Users
Copyright © 2016 by Mark L. Strauss

This title is also available as a Zondervan ebook.

Requests for information should be addressed to:
Zondervan, 3900 *Sparks Dr. SE, Grand Rapids, Michigan 49546*

Library of Congress Cataloging-in-Publication Data

Names: Strauss, Mark L., 1959- author.
Title: The Biblical Greek companion for Bible software users : grammatical terms explained for
    exegesis / Mark L. Strauss.
Description: Grand Rapids, MI : Zondervan, 2016. | Includes bibliographical references and index.
Identifiers: LCCN 2016018455 | ISBN 9780310521341 (paperback)
Subjects: LCSH: Greek language, Biblical—Computer-assisted instruction. | Greek language,
    Biblical—Self-instruction. | Bible—Language, style—Computer-assisted instruction. | Bible—
    Language, style—Programmed instruction.
Classification: LCC PA817 .S78 2016 | DDC 487/.4—dc23 LC record available at https://lccn.loc
    .gov/2016018455

Cover design: FaceOut Studio
Interior design: Kait Lamphere

Printed in the United States of America

16 17 18 19 20 21 22 23 24 25 26 /DCI/ 15 14 13 12 11 10 9 8 7 6 5 4 3 2 1

CONTENTS

INTRODUCTION

Technological advances have provided a remarkable array of resources for those who have an interest in a deeper study of Scripture in its original languages. Programs such as *Logos Bible Software, Accordance Bible Software, BibleWorks*, and others have revolutionized the way we study God's Word. For example, right now I have a Bible software program open on my laptop. I see in parallel columns the Greek text of the passage I am studying, together with three English translations, each providing a slightly different perspective on the meaning of the text. I also have open two electronic commentaries on the passage: when I scroll down in my Bible, the commentaries automatically move to a discussion of those same verses. I no longer need a concordance, since I can type a word—whether in English, Hebrew, or Greek—in a search window and instantly find every use of that word in the Bible. I no longer need my Greek paradigm charts, since I can pass my cursor over any Greek verb and it will instantly parse it for me: tense, voice, mood, person, number. With another click, I can open two or three Greek lexicons that will provide detailed data on the various functions and senses of the word. I can do advanced searches of that word to see every place in which it occurs with other words or phrases. This is remarkable!

Yet while Bible software provides users with an abundance of useful information, it unfortunately does not provide them with an explanation of *what* most of that information means or its significance for understanding biblical texts. For most of us, it has been a long time since we had formal training in English grammar (if we ever had it!). And for those who have studied the biblical languages, much of its terminology is now forgotten. So when a Greek language program informs us, for example, that a word is a vocative, or a genitive, or a subjunctive, or a middle voice, we do not remember (or perhaps have never learned) what these grammatical terms mean.

The Biblical Greek Companion for Bible Software Users provides students—in an alphabetically arranged format—with simple and clear explanations of the basic grammatical terms that they are likely to encounter in their Bible software. To make this resource as user-friendly as possible, each entry provides (1) a description of what the form looks like, (2) a summary of what it does, that is, its main functions (with examples from the Greek New Testament), and (3) an "Exegetical Insight" to show how the grammar will help us interpret the text.

This resource is designed as an aid to anyone who works with New Testament Greek, and especially those who own and use a biblical Greek software program. Intended readers include:

- pastors and other ministry leaders who may have learned biblical Greek at one time, but have experienced the loss of much of that learning because of the time demands of life and ministry;
- college and seminary students who are engaged in a biblical Greek language course, but who could use this resource as a supplement to provide easily accessible and simplified explanations, along with clear biblical examples;
- college and seminary students who are enrolled in an academic program that no longer requires them to learn the biblical languages, but who wish to have access to the wealth of available resources for original-language study;
- those who have never had the opportunity, resources, or inclination to learn the paradigms, vocabulary, grammar, and syntax of biblical Greek, but would still like to benefit from the deeper insights into the Bible that Greek study can provide.

ABBREVIATIONS

acc.	accusative
act.	active
adj.	adjective
adv.	adverb
aor.	aorist
BDAG	Bauer, W. *A Greek-English Lexicon of the New Testament and Other Early Christian Literature.* Translated and revised by W. F. Arndt, F. W. Gingrich, and F. W. Danker. 3rd ed. Chicago: University of Chicago Press, 2000.
BDF	Blass, F., and A. Debrunner. *A Greek Grammar of the New Testament and Other Early Christian Literature.* Translated and revised by R. W. Funk. Chicago: University of Chicago Press, 1961.
BECNT	Baker Exegetical Commentary on the New Testament
CEB	Common English Bible
CEV	Contemporary English Version
dat.	dative
decl.	declension
e.g.	for example
ESV	English Standard Version
fem.	feminine
fut.	future
gen.	genitive
GW	God's Word translation
HCSB	Holman Christian Standard Bible
ind.	indicative
inf.	infinitive
imper.	imperative
impf.	imperfect
KJV	King James Version
masc.	masculine
mid.	middle
NAB	New American Bible
NASB	New American Standard Bible
NCV	New Century Version
NET	New English Translation
neut.	neuter

NIV	New International Version
NJB	New Jerusalem Bible
NKJV	New King James Version
NLT	New Living Translation
NRSV	New Revised Standard Version
nom.	nominative
num.	number (sg./pl.)
opt.	optative
p./pp.	page/pages
part.	participle
pass.	passive
per.	person (1st, 2nd, 3rd)
perf.	perfect
pl.	plural
pres.	present
sg.	singular
subj.	subjunctive
voc.	vocative
Wallace	Wallace, Daniel B. *Greek Grammar Beyond the Basics: An Exegetical Syntax of the New Testament.* Grand Rapids: Zondervan, 1996.
WBC	Word Biblical Commentary

ACCUSATIVE

What It Looks Like

The accusative case is most easily recognized in its singular form by the nun (ν) case ending in the first (-αν, -ην) and second (-ον) declensions (for declension, see NOUN). The plural endings are -ας in the first declension and -ους in the second declension. Third declension masculine and feminine nouns and adjectives end in either nun (-ν) or alpha (-α) in the singular and -ας in the plural. Neuter nouns and adjectives always have the same form in the accusative as the nominative, and neuter plural accusative nouns end in alpha (-α).

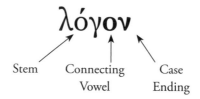

λόγον

Stem   Connecting   Case
Vowel   Ending

Accusative Forms Highlighted

	2nd Decl. Masc.	1st Decl. Fem.	2nd Decl. Neut.	3rd Decl.	3rd Decl. Neut.
Nom. Sg.	λόγος	γραφή	ἔργον	σάρξ	ὄνομα
Gen. Sg.	λόγου	γραφῆς	ἔργου	σαρκός	ὀνόματος
Dat. Sg.	λόγῳ	γραφῇ	ἔργῳ	σαρκί	ὀνόματι
Acc. Sg.	**λόγον**	**γραφήν**	**ἔργον**	**σάρκα**	**ὄνομα**
Nom. Pl.	λόγοι	γραφαί	ἔργα	σάρκες	ὀνόματα
Gen. Pl.	λόγων	γραφῶν	ἔργων	σαρκῶν	ὀνομάτων
Dat. Pl.	λόγοις	γραφαῖς	ἔργοις	σαρξί(ν)	ὀνόμασι(ν)
Acc. Pl.	**λόγους**	**γραφάς**	**ἔργα**	**σάρκας**	**ὀνόματα**

What It Does

The accusative case is one of five cases in Greek—NOMINATIVE, GEN-ITIVE, DATIVE, ACCUSATIVE, and VOCATIVE. Case is the particular form of a noun or substantive that indicates its function. The basic function of the accusative is to measure or define with reference to extent, limitation, scope, or direction. The following are some of its primary functions:

1. *Direct Object.* The most common use of the accusative is as the direct object, which limits or defines the action of the verb.

> Μὴ ἀγαπᾶτε **τὸν κόσμον.**
> "Do not love **the world.**" (1 John 2:15)

2. *Accusative Subject of Infinitive.* When an infinitive has a different subject than the subject of the main verb, the accusative case is used to indicate the subject of the infinitive.

> παρεκάλεσέν τε **τὸν Φίλιππον** ἀναβάντα καθίσαι σὺν αὐτῷ.
> "He invited **Philip** to come up and sit beside him." (Acts 8:31)

3. *Adverbial Accusative of Measure.* A function of the accusative that indicates how far the action of the verb extends in time or space.

> εἶδον τὰ ἔργα μου **τεσσεράκοντα ἔτη.**
> "They saw my works **for forty years.**" (Heb 3:9–10)

4. *Accusative after Certain Prepositions.* Some PREPOSITIONS always take an accusative as their object (εἰς, πρός). Others can take the accusative or other cases (ἐπί, κατά, μετά, περί, ὑπό, παρά).

An Exegetical Insight

One of the more interesting functions of the accusative is the *cognate accusative*, where an accusative noun functions as the direct object of its cognate verb (i.e., it is built on the same root).

> μὴ **θησαυρίζετε** ὑμῖν **θησαυροὺς.**
> "Do not **treasure up treasures** for yourselves." (Matt 6:19)

Cognate accusatives are sometimes used by authors to provide special emphasis for a verb. This is well illustrated in Matthew 2:10: ἐχάρησαν χαρὰν μεγάλην σφόδρα ("They rejoiced exceedingly with great joy."). Emphasis is actually provided here in three ways: (1) with the cognate accusative ("rejoiced with joy"); (2) with the adjective μεγάλη ("great") modifying χαρά ("joy"); and (3) with the adverb σφόδρα ("exceedingly") modifying the verb ἐχάρησαν ("rejoiced").

ACTIVE

What It Looks Like

Since the active voice is a feature of all the verbal moods (INDICATIVE, SUBJUNCTIVE, IMPERATIVE, OPTATIVE) and verbals (PARTICIPLE, INFINITIVE), there are a great many forms the active voice can take. The following are the active forms in the indicative mood. For active forms in other moods and verbals, see their particular entries.

Active Indicative in Various Tenses (verbs: λύω; λείπω)

Present Active Indicative		Future Active Indicative		Imperfect Active Indicative	
Per. Sg.	Pl.	Per. Sg.	Pl.		
1st λύ ω	λύ ο μεν	1st λύ σ ω	λύ σ ομεν	Per. Sg.	Pl.
2nd λύ εις	λύ ε τε	2nd λύ σ εις	λύ σ ε τε	1st ἔ λυ ον	ἐ λύ ομεν
3rd λύ ει	λύ ου σι(ν)	3rd λύ σ ει	λύ σ ουσι(ν)	2nd ἔ λυ ε ς	ἐ λύ ετε
				3rd ἔ λυ ε(ν)	ἔ λυ ον

Perfect Active Indicative		Pluperfect Active Indicative		1st Aorist Active Indicative	
Per. Sg.	Pl.	Per. Sg.	Pl.		
1st λέ λυ κ α	λε λύ κ α μεν	1st ἐ λε λύ κ ει ν	ἐ λε λύ κ ει μεν	Per. Sg.	Pl.
2nd λέ λυ κ ας	λε λύ κ α τε	2nd ἐ λε λύ κ ει ς	ἐ λε λύ κ ει τε	1st ἔ λυ σ α	ἐ λύ σ α μεν
3rd λέ λυ κ ε(ν)	λε λύ κ α ν	3rd ἐ λε λύ κ ει	ἐ λε λύ κ ει σαν	2nd ἔ λυ σ ας	ἐ λύ σ α τε
	(-κασι[ν])			3rd ἔ λυ σ ε(ν)	ἔ λυ σ α ν

				2nd Aorist Active Indicative	
				Per. Sg.	Pl.
				1st ἔ λιπ ον	ἐ λίπ ομεν
				2nd ἔ λιπ ες	ἐ λίπ ετε
				3rd ἔ λιπ ε(ν)	ἔ λιπ ον
				(λείπω = leave, forsake)	

What It Does

Voice indicates the relationship of the subject of a sentence to its VERB, whether it is *acting* or *being acted upon*. The active voice indicates that the subject is doing the action. There are various functions of the active voice:

1. *Simple Active.* The subject directly performs the action.

> τὸ φῶς ἐν τῇ σκοτίᾳ **φαίνει.**
> "The light **shines** in the darkness." (John 1:5)

τοῦτον τὸν Ἰησοῦν **ἀνέστησεν** ὁ θεός.
"God **raised** this Jesus to life." (Acts 2:32)

ἐγὼ **ἐφύτευσα**, Ἀπολλῶς **ἐπότισεν**, ἀλλ᾽ ὁ θεὸς ηὔξανεν.
"**I planted**, Apollos **watered**, but God caused the growth." (1 Cor 3:6)

2. *Causative Active*. The subject indirectly causes the action.

τὸν ἥλιον αὐτοῦ **ἀνατέλλει** ἐπὶ πονηροὺς καὶ ἀγαθούς.
"**He causes** his sun **to rise** on the evil and the good." (Matt 5:45)

εἰ βρῶμα **σκανδαλίζει** τὸν ἀδελφόν μου . . .
"If food **causes** my brother **to sin** . . ." (1 Cor 8:13)

ἐγὼ ἐφύτευσα, Ἀπολλῶς ἐπότισεν, ἀλλ᾽ ὁ θεὸς **ηὔξανεν**.
"I planted, Apollos watered, but God **caused the growth**." (1 Cor 3:6)

3. *Stative Active*. Rather than acting, the subject is *equated* with a thing or with a state of being.

Ἐγώ **εἰμι** ἡ ἄμπελος ἡ ἀληθινὴ καὶ ὁ πατήρ μου ὁ γεωργός **ἐστιν**.
"**I am** the true vine, and my Father **is** the gardener." (John 15:1)

σὺ **εἶ** ὁ υἱός μου ὁ ἀγαπητός, ἐν σοὶ **εὐδόκησα**.
"**You are** my Son, whom I love; with you **I am well pleased**." (Luke 3:22)

An Exegetical Insight

A good example of a causative active is found in John 19:1:

Τότε οὖν ἔλαβεν ὁ Πιλᾶτος τὸν Ἰησοῦν καὶ **ἐμαστίγωσεν**.
"Then Pilate took Jesus and **flogged** him." (John 19:1)

Pilate would not have taken part in the actual flogging, but it was conducted under his orders. Most actions of rulers are by their nature causative actives, since their orders are carried out by subordinates. "Herod . . . killed all the children in Bethlehem . . . two years old and younger" (Ἡρῴδης . . . ἀνεῖλεν πάντας τοὺς παῖδας τοὺς ἐν Βηθλέεμ . . . ἀπὸ διετοῦς καὶ κατωτέρω; Matt 2:16); Herod Antipas "seizing John, bound him and put him in prison" (κρατήσας τὸν Ἰωάννην ἔδησεν αὐτὸν καὶ ἐν φυλακῇ ἀπέθετο; Matt 14:3); Herod Agrippa "killed James the brother of John with the sword" (ἀνεῖλεν δὲ Ἰάκωβον τὸν ἀδελφὸν Ἰωάννου μαχαίρῃ; Acts 12:2). All of these actions were performed by soldiers under the orders of a ruler who was ultimately responsible for the action.

ADJECTIVE

What It Looks Like

Adjectives decline in the same three declensions as nouns and have similar endings (for declension, see NOUN). Like nouns, every adjective is identified in terms of *case, number,* and *gender.* While nouns have one gender (masculine, feminine, or neuter), adjectives must be able to change their gender in order to agree with the noun or substantive they modify.

Most adjectives decline in the second declension in the masculine and neuter and in the first declension in the feminine (these are called 2-1-2 adjectives; see ἀγαθός below). Others decline in the third declension in the masculine and neuter and first declension in the feminine (3-1-3 adjectives; see πᾶς below). Still others decline entirely in the second declension (2-2; e.g., ἁμαρτωλός) or entirely in the third declension (3-3; e.g., τις).

ἀγαθός ("good") 2-1-2				πᾶς ("all") 3-1-3			
	masc. 2	fem. 1	neut. 2		masc. 3	fem. 1	neut. 3
Nom. Sg.	ἀγαθός	ἀγαθή	ἀγαθόν	Nom. Sg.	πᾶς	πᾶσα	πᾶν
Gen. Sg.	ἀγαθοῦ	ἀγαθῆς	ἀγαθοῦ	Gen. Sg.	παντός	πάσης	παντός
Dat. Sg.	ἀγαθῷ	ἀγαθῇ	ἀγαθῷ	Dat. Sg.	παντί	πάσῃ	παντί
Acc. Sg.	ἀγαθόν	ἀγαθήν	ἀγαθόν	Acc. Sg.	πάντα	πᾶσαν	πᾶν
Nom. Pl.	ἀγαθοί	ἀγαθαί	ἀγαθά	Nom. Pl.	πάντες	πᾶσαι	πάντα
Gen. Pl.	ἀγαθῶν	ἀγαθῶν	ἀγαθῶν	Gen. Pl.	πάντων	πασῶν	πάντων
Dat. Pl.	ἀγαθοῖς	ἀγαθαῖς	ἀγαθοῖς	Dat. Pl.	πᾶσι(ν)	πάσαις	πᾶσι(ν)
Acc. Pl.	ἀγαθούς	ἀγαθάς	ἀγαθά	Acc. Pl.	πάντας	πάσας	πάντα

What It Does

An adjective is a word that modifies or qualifies a noun or other substantive. Common Greek adjectives include words like πολύς ("many," "much"), μέγας ("great"), ἅγιος ("holy"), καλός ("good"). Adjectives can be identified in terms of *degree:* (1) *Positive,* providing a noun with an attribute ("great"). (2) *Comparative,* comparing two or more things ("greater"). (3) *Superlative,* expressing the ultimate degree ("greatest"). They can also be identified in terms of their function in the sentence. There are three main functions of adjectives:

1. *Attributive Adjective.* The adjective provides a noun with an attribute.

> ἦν ἀνὴρ **ἀγαθὸς** καὶ πλήρης πνεύματος **ἁγίου**.
> "He was a **good** man and full of the **Holy** Spirit." (Acts 11:24)

2. *Substantival Adjective.* The adjective functions as a noun.

> τί **ἀγαθὸν** ποιήσω ἵνα σχῶ ζωὴν αἰώνιον;
> "What **good thing** must I do to have eternal life?" (Matt 19:16)

3. *Predicate Adjective.* The adjective in the predicate describes an attribute of the subject. A copulative (equative) verb like εἰμί is either present or implied.

> οὗτος ἔσται **μέγας**.
> "He will be **great**." (Luke 1:32)

Other parts of speech can also function as adjectives. When a word, phrase, or clause modifies a noun, it is said to be functioning *adjectivally.* Relative clauses (see PRONOUN, RELATIVE) and participial phrases (see PARTICIPLE) often function adjectivally in Greek. For example, in the phrase, ἄνθρωπος ὃς ἦν παραλελυμένος ("a man who was paralyzed"), the relative clause ὃς ἦν παραλελυμένος ("who was paralyzed") is functioning adjectivally, modifying the noun ἄνθρωπος ("man").

An Exegetical Insight

In Koine Greek, the force of the positive, comparative, and superlative adjectives often overlaps. For example, the positive is sometimes used for the comparative. In Mark 9:43, the positive adjective καλός ("good") clearly means "better":

> **καλόν** ἐστίν σε κυλλὸν εἰσελθεῖν εἰς τὴν ζωὴν ἢ τὰς δύο χεῖρας ἔχοντα ἀπελθεῖν εἰς τὴν γέενναν.
> "It is **better** for you to enter life crippled than with two hands to enter hell." (Mark 9:43)

Similarly, the positive can be used for the superlative. In Luke 9:48, the positive adjective μέγας ("great") means "greatest":

> ὁ γὰρ μικρότερος ἐν πᾶσιν ὑμῖν ὑπάρχων οὗτός ἐστιν **μέγας**.
> "For it is the least among you all who is the **greatest**." (Luke 9:48)

It is important to identify the sense of the adjective in context and translate accordingly.

ADVERB

What It Looks Like

Greek adverbs have no distinguishing features that differentiate them from other kinds of words. Unlike nouns, adjectives, and verbs, they do not decline or have inflection (i.e., they do not change their form).

The following are some of the most common adverbs in the Greek New Testament:

Adverb	Meaning	Occurrences
οὕτως	thus, so, in this way	208
καθώς	as, just as, inasmuch as	182
τότε	then, when, at that time	158
νῦν	now, as it is, in fact	140
πάλιν	again, once more	136
ἐκεῖ	there, in a place where	105
ἔτι	yet, still, again	82
μᾶλλον	more, rather, instead	79
ἔξω	outside	62
πρῶτον	first, earlier, above all	60
ὧδε	here	59
ἤδη	now, already	56
εὐθύς	immediately, next, suddenly	50
οὐκέτι	no longer, not again	45

What It Does

Greek adverbs function like English adverbs: they modify or qualify verbs, adjectives, or other adverbs. Adverbs in English are words like "quickly," "sadly," "often," "there," "then." "Adverbial" refers to a word, phrase, or clause that functions like an adverb, that is, it modifies a verb, an adjective, or another adverb. In addition to adverbs themselves, participles, prepositional phrases, and subordinate clauses can function adverbially.

Adverbs and adverbial phrases indicate functions like time, place, manner, mode, means, degree, purpose, cause, etc. They answer questions like *When? Where? How? How much? Why?* etc. with reference to the word or phrase they are modifying. For example, in the sentence, "He ran *quickly*," the adverb "quickly" answers the question "how" with reference to *ran*.

The following list explains some common adverbial functions:

1. *Temporal.* Answers the question, "*When?*"

   Τότε οἱ μαθηταὶ πάντες ἀφέντες αὐτὸν ἔφυγον.
   "**Then** all the disciples deserted him and fled." (Matt 26:56)

2. *Place.* Answers "*Where?*"

   πᾶν τὸ πλῆθος ἦν τοῦ λαοῦ προσευχόμενον **ἔξω.**
   "The whole assembly of the people was praying **outside.**" (Luke 1:10)

3. *Modal.* Answers "*How?*"

   τί οὗτος **οὕτως** λαλεῖ; βλασφημεῖ·
   "Why does this man speak **in this way?** He blasphemes!" (Mark 2:7)

An Exegetical Insight

There are a relatively small number of adverbs in the New Testament (3,645) compared to other parts of speech. The reason for this, however, is that so many other parts of speech function *adverbially*, modifying verbs, adjectives, or other adverbs. Consider the following clause from Ephesians 1:

ἐξελέξατο ἡμᾶς ἐν αὐτῷ πρὸ καταβολῆς κόσμου εἶναι ἡμᾶς ἁγίους καὶ ἀμώμους κατενώπιον αὐτοῦ ἐν ἀγάπῃ.
"He chose us in him before the foundation of the world, for us to be holy and blameless before him in love." (Eph 1:4)

Although there are no adverbs in this verse, there are many things functioning *adverbially*, modifying the verb ἐξελέξατο ("he chose us"). The prepositional phrase ἐν αὐτῷ ("in him") tells us *where* he chose us to be. The prepositional phrase πρὸ καταβολῆς κόσμου ("before the foundation of the world") tells us *when* he chose us; the infinitival phrase εἶναι ἡμᾶς ἁγίους καὶ ἀμώμους ("for us to be holy and blameless") tells us *why* he chose us. There is profound theological truth in these adverbial phrases.

AORIST

What It Looks Like

Aorists follow two different patterns, first aorists and second aorists. There is no difference in meaning between the two patterns. First aorists are "regular" aorists. They are formed by adding the aorist tense formative sigma (-σ), a connecting vowel (usually α), followed by secondary personal endings (the endings on aorist, imperfect, and perfect verbs). Second aorists are irregular stem aorists. Instead of -σα endings, they have the same endings as the IMPERFECT tense endings in the INDICATIVE mood and the PRESENT tense endings in other moods. But there is always a change in stem form from the present tense stem (the first principal part; see VERB). In the INDICATIVE mood, aorists have an epsilon augment (ἐ-) at the beginning of the verb. Outside the indicative, there is no augment.

First Aorist Active Indicative (1st person plural; verb λύω)

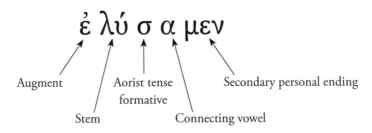

ἐ λύ σ α μεν

Augment / Aorist tense formative / Secondary personal ending
Stem / Connecting vowel

Aorist Indicative Forms (verbs: λύω; λείπω)

		1ˢᵗ Aorist (λύω)			2ⁿᵈ Aorist (λείπω)	
Active	Per.	Sg.	Pl.	Per.	Sg.	Pl.
	1ˢᵗ	ἔ λυ σ α	ἐ λύ σ α μεν	1ˢᵗ	ἔ λιπ ον	ἐ λίπ ομεν
	2ⁿᵈ	ἔ λυ σ α ς	ἐ λύ σ α τε	2ⁿᵈ	ἔ λιπ ες	ἐ λίπ ετε
	3ʳᵈ	ἔ λυ σ ε(ν)	ἔ λυ σ α ν	3ʳᵈ	ἔ λιπ ε(ν)	ἔ λιπ ον
Middle	Per.	Sg.	Pl.	Per.	Sg.	Pl.
	1ˢᵗ	ἐλυ σά μην	ἐ λυ σ ά μεθα	1ˢᵗ	ἐ λιπ ό μην	ἐ λιπ ό μεθα
	2ⁿᵈ	ἐ λύ σ ω	ἐ λύ σ α σθε	2ⁿᵈ	ἐ λίπ ου	ἐ λίπ ε σθε
	3ʳᵈ	ἐ λύ σ α το	ἐ λύ σ α ντο	3ʳᵈ	ἐ λίπ ε το	ἐ λίπ ο ντο
Passive	Per.	Sg.	Pl.	Per.	Sg.	Pl.
	1ˢᵗ	ἐ λύ θη ν	ἐ λύ θη μεν	1ˢᵗ	ἐ λίπ η ν	ἐ λίπ η μεν
	2ⁿᵈ	ἐ λύ θη ς	ἐ λύ θη τε	2ⁿᵈ	ἐ λίπ η ς	ἐ λίπ η τε
	3ʳᵈ	ἐ λύ θη	ἐ λύ θη σαν	3ʳᵈ	ἔ λιπ η	ἐ λίπ η σαν

What It Does

Tense in Greek can indicate the *time* of an action as well as *aspect,* the kind of action (see VERB). Aspect is always primary. Time becomes a factor only in the INDICATIVE mood, where the aorist usually indicates simple past time: "he ran." This can be contrasted with the IMPERFECT tense, which indicates continuous or progressive past action ("he was running") and the PERFECT tense, which indicates completed past action ("he has run"). Outside the indicative mood, the aorist signifies only aspect. The aorist aspect is *perfective,* referring to the action from the outside, as a whole, without reference to its beginning or end. By analogy, the aorist is sometimes described as a snapshot of the action, while the imperfect is a motion picture, portraying the action as it unfolds.[1] The following are some of the common functions of the aorist:

1. *Constative Aorist.* Views the action in its entirety, without reference to its beginning, end, or duration. This is the most basic function of the aorist.

   οἱ πατέρες ἡμῶν ἐν τῷ ὄρει τούτῳ **προσεκύνησαν.**
   "Our ancestors **worshiped** on this mountain." (John 4:20)

2. *Ingressive Aorist.* Stresses the beginning of an action or entrance into a new state.

   ὁ ἀδελφός σου οὗτος νεκρὸς ἦν καὶ **ἔζησεν.**
   "This brother of yours was dead, and **has come back to life.**" (Luke 15:32)

3. *Consummative Aorist.* Stresses the end or cessation of an action.

   ἐνίκησεν ὁ λέων ὁ ἐκ τῆς φυλῆς Ἰούδα.
   "The lion of the tribe of Judah **has prevailed.**" (Rev 5:5)

An Exegetical Insight

Consider the use of the aorist in Romans 3:23:

πάντες γὰρ **ἥμαρτον** καὶ ὑστεροῦνται τῆς δόξης τοῦ θεοῦ.
"For all [**have**] **sinned** and fall short of the glory of God."

The aorist ἥμαρτον (from ἁμαρτάνω) could mean everyone has sinned at some point in the past, or that all sin repeatedly, or that everyone is a sinner. The aorist simply states the reality of the action, without identifying it as a single act, a completed act, or a continuous act. The aorist here likely stresses the reality of the sinfulness of humanity rather than to point to particular acts of sin.

---

1. Wallace, *Grammar,* 554–55.

──────── ARTICLE ────────

What It Looks Like

The Greek article is similar in form to the endings of first and second declension nouns and adjectives (see NOUN, ADJECTIVE). The MASCULINE and FEMININE forms of the NOMINATIVE have a rough breathing mark (ʽ = an "h" sound). All other forms begin with a tau (τ).

CASE	Singular			Plural		
	Masc.	Fem.	Neut.	Masc.	Fem.	Neut.
Nom.	ὁ	ἡ	τό	οἱ	αἱ	τά
Gen.	τοῦ	τῆς	τοῦ	τῶν	τῶν	τῶν
Dat.	τῷ	τῇ	τῷ	τοῖς	ταῖς	τοῖς
Acc.	τόν	τήν	τό	τούς	τάς	τά

What It Does

Whereas English has a definite article ("the") and an indefinite article ("a/an"), Greek has only a single article, which functions very differently from the English article. The primary role of the Greek article is *not* to make something definite ("the"). Many nouns in Greek are definite without the article. The article's primary function is rather to *conceptualize* or *identify* things. For example, the article can *nominalize* something, that is, turn it into a substantive (= make it function like a noun). The adjective ἀγαθός ("good") can be turned into a substantive with the article: ὁ ἀγαθός ("the good person"). This is a powerful function in Greek, since the article can turn practically anything into a substantive (or an adjective). For example, in the phrase ὁ ἐν τῷ ἀγρῷ (Matt 24:18), the article ὁ turns the prepositional phrase ἐν τῷ ἀγρῷ ("in the field") into a substantive: "the in-the-field one," that is, "the one who is in the field."

In addition to conceptualizing things, the article often points things out. Commonly in Greek, the first reference to a person will not have the article: παραγίνεται **Ἰωάννης** ὁ βαπτιστὴς κηρύσσων ἐν τῇ ἐρήμῳ τῆς Ἰουδαίας ("John the Baptist came, preaching in the wilderness of Judea"; Matt 3:1), while the second will: ὁ **Ἰωάννης** εἶχεν τὸ ἔνδυμα αὐτοῦ ἀπὸ τριχῶν καμήλου. ("*This* John [the one just referred to] had a garment made from camel's hair"; Matt 3:4). This is called the anaphoric use of the article (cf. Matt 27:2, 13).

The article agrees with the word that it modifies in case, number, and gender.

An Exegetical Insight

One of the most discussed and debated uses of the article in the New Testament is John 1:1:

Ἐν ἀρχῇ ἦν ὁ λόγος, καὶ ὁ λόγος ἦν πρὸς τὸν θεόν, καὶ **θεὸς** ἦν ὁ λόγος.

"In the beginning was the Word, and the Word was with God, and the Word was **God**."

Some groups, such as the Jehovah's Witnesses, claim that "God" should be translated "a god," because of the absence of the article before θεός.

This is unlikely for the following reasons:

1. The lack of article does not indicate indefiniteness. Thousands of anarthrous (= without the article) nouns in the New Testament are definite. Many others are *qualitative* but not indefinite. Rules related to the Greek article are complex, but in general, the article indicates *identity* and the lack of article, *quality*.

2. Predicate nominatives in Greek are often anarthrous *to distinguish them from the subject*. The article in front of ὁ λόγος indicates that it is the subject of the final clause θεὸς ἦν ὁ λόγος. The lack of article on θεός indicates it is the predicate nominative.

3. Colwell's Rule states that, "A definite noun preceding a copulative verb is usually anarthrous." (See details in Wallace, *Grammar*, 256–70.) Consider John 1:49: ῥαββί, σὺ εἶ **ὁ υἱὸς** τοῦ θεοῦ, σὺ **βασιλεὺς** εἶ τοῦ Ἰσραήλ. ("Rabbi, you are the Son of God; you are the king of Israel."). The predicate nominative ὁ υἱός has the article because it is *after the verb*. The predicate nominative βασιλεύς is anarthrous because it is *before the verb*. Applied to John 1:1, if θεός *is definite or qualitative,* it is *normal* for it to lack the article.

   While Colwell's rule has been misused to claim that anarthrous predicate nouns that precede a copulative verb *are always definite* (the rule states instead that *if* these nouns are definite, they are usually anarthrous), subsequent research has shown that most of these preverbal anarthrous predicate nominatives are *qualitative* or *definite,* not indefinite.

4. Elsewhere throughout John's prologue, θεός is used without the article to mean "God," not "a god" (John 1:6, 12, 13, 18; cf. John 3:2, 21; 6:45; 9:16, 33). John 1:18 is particularly telling, since it says, "No one has ever seen God" (Θεὸν οὐδεὶς ἑώρακεν πώποτε), clearly referring to God the Father. Yet there is no article before θεός.

CONJUNCTION, CONDITIONAL

What It Looks Like

The most common conditional conjunctions in Greek are εἰ and ἐάν, both of which mean "if." The former is used primarily with the INDICATIVE mood; the latter with the SUBJUNCTIVE mood.

What It Does

Conditional conjunctions are conjunctions that introduce conditional clauses. Conditional clauses are subordinate clauses that express the conditions under which the action of the main clause takes place (see also CONJUNCTION, SUBORDINATE). Conditional clauses in English commonly begin with "if." A conditional sentence contains two parts, the *protasis* (the "if . . ." part of the sentence; the conditional clause), the *apodosis* (the "then . . ." part of the sentence; this is the main clause). *Example*: "If you study hard [*protasis*], you will do well on the final exam [*apodosis*]." The protasis is the condition under which the apodosis is achieved.

There are four main types of conditional clauses in Greek:

1. *First class conditions* ("conditions of fact") assume (for the sake of the argument) that if something is true, then something else will follow. Protasis: εἰ + INDICATIVE mood. Apodosis: any mood; any tense.

   εἰ γὰρ κατὰ σάρκα ζῆτε, μέλλετε ἀποθνήσκειν.
   "For if you live according to the flesh, you will die." (Rom 8:13)

2. *Second class conditions* ("contrary to fact") assume (for the sake of the argument) that if something were true—even though it is not—then something else would follow. Protasis: εἰ + INDICATIVE mood in the aorist or imperfect tense. Apodosis: ἄν + the indicative in the same tense (aorist or imperfect).

   εἰ γὰρ ἐπιστεύετε Μωϋσεῖ, ἐπιστεύετε ἄν ἐμοί.
   "If you believed Moses, you would believe me." (John 5:46)

3. *Third class conditions* present a condition that might be true in the future or is generally true at all times. Protasis: ἐάν + SUBJUNCTIVE mood. Apodosis: any mood; any tense.

ἐὰν δὲ ἀποθάνῃ ὁ ἀνήρ, κατήργηται ἀπὸ τοῦ νόμου τοῦ ἀνδρός.
"But if her husband dies, she is released from the law of marriage." (Rom 7:2)

4. *Fourth class conditions* express a possible condition in the future, usually one which is remote. Protasis: εἰ + OPTATIVE mood. Apodosis: ἄν + optative mood. There are no complete examples of this in the New Testament (that is, examples that have *both* a protasis and an apodosis).

εἰ καὶ πάσχοιτε διὰ δικαιοσύνην, μακάριοι.
"Even if you should suffer because of righteousness, [you will be] blessed." (1 Pet 3:14)

An Exegetical Insight

A good example of a second class (contrary-to-fact) condition appears in Luke 7:39. In Luke 7:36–49, Jesus is dining in the home of a Pharisee named Simon when a woman with a sinful reputation comes in. She anoints Jesus's feet with expensive perfume, kisses them, wets them with her tears, and wipes them with her hair. Simon is appalled that Jesus would allow such a woman to touch him, and he thinks to himself:

εἰ ἦν προφήτης, ἐγίνωσκεν ἄν τίς καὶ ποταπὴ ἡ γυνὴ ἥτις ἅπτεται αὐτοῦ, ὅτι ἁμαρτωλός ἐστιν.
"If he were a prophet, he would know who is touching him and what kind of woman she is—that she is a sinner." (Luke 7:39)

The conditional clause, "If he were a prophet . . ." is a second class condition (εἰ + indicative in the protasis; ἄν + indicative in the apodosis), indicating that Simon is assuming that Jesus is *not* in fact a prophet.

The irony of the scene is that Jesus immediately detects Simon's thoughts—the mark of a true prophet! He then tells him a parable about the appropriate response to God's grace (Luke 7:41–43). The woman, who has experienced great forgiveness, responds to Jesus with great love. But Simon, who does not feel any need for forgiveness, has not shown Jesus even the most basic signs of love and hospitality. The conclusion: those who experience God's overwhelming love and grace will respond with great love and gratitude.

CONJUNCTION, COORDINATE

What It Looks Like

The most common coordinate conjunctions in Greek are καί ("and") and δέ ("and" or "but"), but there are several others (see below).

What It Does

Conjunctions are words used to connect clauses or sentences, or to coordinate words in the same clause (English conjunctions include words such as *and, but, if,* etc.). *Coordinate* conjunctions join words, phrases, or clauses of *equal grammatical rank*. (See also CONJUNCTIONS, SUBORDINATE). There are six main types of coordinate conjunctions: continuative, adversative, correlative, disjunctive, explanatory, and inferential.

1. *Continuative.* The most common type of coordinate conjunction, it connects an additional element to a series. The most common are καί and δέ.

   ἐπὶ τῆς Μωϋσέως καθέδρας ἐκάθισαν οἱ γραμματεῖς **καὶ** οἱ Φαρισαῖοι.
   "The scribes **and** the Pharisees sit in Moses's seat." (Matt 23:2)

2. *Adversative.* Also known as contrasting conjunctions, these conjunctions are used to express comparisons or contrasts. English adversative conjunctions include "but," "rather," "yet," "though." The most common adversative conjunction in Greek is ἀλλά ("but," "on the contrary"; 603x). δέ and καί function as adversatives in many contexts.

   καὶ μὴ εἰσενέγκῃς ἡμᾶς εἰς πειρασμόν, **ἀλλὰ** ῥῦσαι ἡμᾶς ἀπὸ τοῦ πονηροῦ.
   "And do not lead us into temptation, **but** deliver us from the evil one." (Matt 6:13)

3. *Correlative.* Two conjunctions that pair up to indicate the relationship between various elements in a sentence. Sometimes the correlative sense is implicit in English and need not be explicitly expressed.

   Ἰωάννης **μὲν** ἐβάπτισεν ὕδατι, ὑμεῖς **δὲ** ἐν πνεύματι βαπτισθήσεσθε ἁγίῳ.
   "**[On the one hand]** John baptized with water, **but [on the other]** you will be baptized with the Holy Spirit." (Acts 1:5)

4. *Disjunctive.* Coordinate conjunctions that are used to separate two alternate possibilities, usually translated "or." A disjunctive conjunction usually

indicates that only one of the options is true or that neither is true. The most common disjunctive conjunction in Greek is ἤ ("or").

τὸ βάπτισμα τὸ Ἰωάννου ἐξ οὐρανοῦ ἦν **ἢ** ἐξ ἀνθρώπων;
"John's baptism—was it from heaven **or** of human origin?" (Mark 11:30)

5. *Explanatory.* A type of coordinate conjunction that indicates additional information is being given about the topic under discussion. The most common explanatory conjunction in the NT is γάρ ("for").

ἀγαπητοὶ διὰ τοὺς πατέρας· ἀμεταμέλητα **γὰρ** τὰ χαρίσματα καὶ ἡ κλῆσις τοῦ θεοῦ.
"they are loved on account of the patriarchs, **for** God's gifts and his call are irrevocable." (Rom 11:28–29)

6. *Inferential.* A type of coordinate conjunction that introduces an inference, deduction, or conclusion. These are often translated, "therefore." Common inferential conjunctions in Greek are ἄρα, διό, and οὖν.

Δικαιωθέντες **οὖν** ἐκ πίστεως εἰρήνην ἔχομεν πρὸς τὸν θεὸν διὰ τοῦ κυρίου ἡμῶν Ἰησοῦ Χριστοῦ.
"**Therefore**, having been justified by faith, we have peace with God through our Lord Jesus Christ." (Rom 5:1)

An Exegetical Insight

Inferential conjunctions in the New Testament often carry profound theological significance, by pointing to the consequence or result of God's work in human history. For example, Romans 12:1 begins Παρακαλῶ **οὖν** ὑμᾶς, ἀδελφοί, διὰ τῶν οἰκτιρμῶν τοῦ θεοῦ ("**Therefore**, I urge you brothers and sister, on account of God's mercies . . ."). The "therefore" (οὖν) here looks back to Paul's masterful discussion throughout Romans 1–11 of God's saving work through his Son and the Spirit. In light of God's overwhelming grace, the only appropriate response is παραστῆσαι τὰ σώματα ὑμῶν θυσίαν ζῶσαν ἁγίαν εὐάρεστον τῷ θεῷ, τὴν λογικὴν λατρείαν ὑμῶν ("to offer your bodies as a living sacrifice, holy and pleasing to God—this is your true and proper worship").

CONJUNCTION, SUBORDINATE

What It Looks Like

The most common subordinate conjunctions are ὅτι ("because," "that"; 1,294x) and ἵνα ("in order that," "so that"; 663x), but there are many others.

What It Does

Subordinate conjunctions are conjunctions that join an independent (main) clause with a dependent (subordinate) clause. (See also CONJUNCTIONS, COORDINATE). There are various kinds of subordinate conjunctions:

1. *Causal conjunctions* introduce subordinate causal clauses, which identify the cause or reason for the action of the main verb. The most common are ὅτι, γάρ, διότι, and ἐπεί.

    > εὐχαριστῶ τῷ θεῷ μου . . . **ὅτι** ἡ πίστις ὑμῶν καταγγέλλεται ἐν ὅλῳ τῷ κόσμῳ.
    > "I thank my God . . . **because** your faith is being reported throughout the whole world." (Rom. 1:8)

2. *Comparative conjunctions* introduce subordinate clauses that draw a comparison to the action of the main clause. The most common are ὡς and καθώς.

    > Βλέπετε οὖν ἀκριβῶς πῶς περιπατεῖτε μὴ **ὡς** ἄσοφοι ἀλλ᾽ ὡς σοφοί.
    > "Therefore be very careful how you live, not **as** unwise people but as wise." (Eph 5:15)

3. *Concessive conjunctions* introduce subordinate clauses that concede something related to the main clause or that express something despite which the action of the main clause occurred.

    > ἡμεῖς γάρ ἐσμεν ἡ περιτομή, οἱ . . . οὐκ ἐν σαρκὶ πεποιθότες, **καίπερ** ἐγὼ ἔχων πεποίθησιν καὶ ἐν σαρκί.
    > "For we are the circumcision, who . . . put no confidence in the flesh— **though** I myself have reasons for such confidence in the flesh." (Phil 3:3–4)

4. *Purpose conjunctions* introduce subordinate clauses that describe the purpose, reason, goal, or aim for an action or event. The most common is ἵνα.

ἀλλὰ τὰ μωρὰ τοῦ κόσμου ἐξελέξατο ὁ θεός, **ἵνα** καταισχύνῃ τοὺς σοφούς.
"But God chose the foolish things of the world **in order to** shame the wise."
(1 Cor 1:27)

5. *Resultative conjunctions* introduce subordinate clauses that describe the result of an action or event. The most common is ὥστε.

   τὰ κύματα ἐπέβαλλεν εἰς τὸ πλοῖον, **ὥστε** ἤδη γεμίζεσθαι τὸ πλοῖον.
   "The waves broke over the boat, **so that** the boat was nearly swamped."
   (Mark 4:37)

6. *Temporal conjunctions* introduce subordinate temporal clauses, which indicate the time of an action or event. Common temporal conjunctions and prepositions include ὅτε/ὅταν, ἕως, πρίν, ἄχρι, μέχρι, and ὡς.

   καὶ **ὅταν** προσεύχησθε, οὐκ ἔσεσθε ὡς οἱ ὑποκριταί.
   "And **when** you pray, do not be like the hypocrites." (Matt 6:5)

An Exegetical Insight

The most common subordinate conjunction in the New Testament in ὅτι, which introduces not only causal clauses but a variety of other clauses, including direct and indirect discourse. In English, we distinguish these two by their form. While English uses "that" for indirect discourse and quotation marks for direct, Greek uses the ὅτι for both.

λέγει αὐτῇ ὁ Ἰησοῦς· καλῶς εἶπας **ὅτι ἄνδρα οὐκ ἔχω·**
Jesus said to her, "Correctly you have said, '**I do not have a husband.**'" (John 4:17)

This is direct discourse. By contrast:

ὁ ἄνθρωπος . . . ἀνήγγειλεν τοῖς Ἰουδαίοις **ὅτι Ἰησοῦς ἐστιν ὁ ποιήσας αὐτὸν ὑγιῆ.**
The man . . . announced to the Jewish leaders **that Jesus was the one who made him well.** (John 5:15)

This is indirect discourse, since direct discourse would have read, "Jesus was the one who made *me* well."

DATIVE

What It Looks Like

The dative case is formed in the singular by the addition of iota (ι) to the connecting vowel. In the second declension (omicron stem; for declension see NOUN), the omicron lengthens to an omega and the iota subscripts (-ῳ). In the first declension (alpha and eta stem), the iota subscripts (-ᾳ or -ῃ). In the third declension (consonantal stem), the iota remains (e.g., σάρκι). The plural endings are -αις in the first declension and -οις in the second declension. In the third declension the plural ending is -σι(ν). This is sometimes altered because of the collision between the sigma and the consonantal ending (e.g. σαρκ + -σιν = σαρξίν).

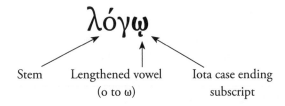

| | Stem | Lengthened vowel (o to ω) | Iota case ending subscript |

Dative Forms Highlighted

	2nd Decl. Masc.	1st Decl. Fem.	2nd Decl. Neut.	3rd Decl.	3rd Decl. Neut.
Nom. Sg.	λόγος	γραφή	ἔργον	σάρξ	ὄνομα
Gen. Sg.	λόγου	γραφῆς	ἔργου	σαρκός	ὀνόματος
Dat. Sg.	**λόγῳ**	**γραφῇ**	**ἔργῳ**	**σαρκί**	**ὀνόματι**
Acc. Sg.	λόγον	γραφήν	ἔργον	σάρκα	ὄνομα
Nom. Pl.	λόγοι	γραφαί	ἔργα	σάρκες	ὀνόματα
Gen. Pl.	λόγων	γραφῶν	ἔργων	σαρκῶν	ὀνομάτων
Dat. Pl.	**λόγοις**	**γραφαῖς**	**ἔργοις**	**σαρξί(ν)**	**ὀνόμασι(ν)**
Acc. Pl.	λόγους	γραφάς	ἔργα	σάρκας	ὀνόματα

What It Does

The DATIVE case is one of five Greek cases. The others are NOMINATIVE, GENITIVE, ACCUSATIVE, and VOCATIVE. Case is the particular form of a noun or substantive that indicates its function. At its most basic, the dative is the case of reference, respect, or personal interest. It is commonly translated with words like *in, to, at, by, with*. Here are some of its common functions:

1. *Indirect Object*. The most common function of the dative.

   δεδώκει δὲ ὁ παραδιδοὺς αὐτὸν σύσσημον **αὐτοῖς**.
   "The betrayer gave **them** a signal." (Mark 14:44)

2. *Dative of Advantage or Disadvantage*. Indicates a person or persons for whose benefit something is done, or against whom something is done.

   γινώσκετε τί πεποίηκα **ὑμῖν**;
   "Do you understand what I have done **for you**?" (John 13:12)

   μαρτυρεῖτε **ἑαυτοῖς**.
   "You testify **against yourselves**." (Matt 23:31)

3. *Dative of Reference/Respect*. Limits or qualifies with respect to what or whom something is true.

   μὴ μεριμνᾶτε **τῇ ψυχῇ** ὑμῶν.
   "Do not be anxious **with respect to** your **life**." (Matt 6:25)

4. *Dative of Means/Instrument*. Indicates the means by which the action is accomplished.

   ἐναρξάμενοι **πνεύματι** νῦν **σαρκὶ** ἐπιτελεῖσθε;
   "After beginning **by means of the Spirit**, are you now trying to finish **by means of the flesh?**" (Gal 3:3)

An Exegetical Insight

The basic nature of the cases can be illustrated by how each case functions to express time. The accusative, genitive, and dative cases can all function temporally, but in different ways. The *dative of time* commonly indicates *a point of time*, since the dative is the case of reference: τῇ δὲ μιᾷ τῶν σαββάτων ("**On the first day** of the week"; Luke 24:1). The *genitive of time* usually indicates *kind* or quality of time, since the genitive is the descriptive case: ἦλθεν πρὸς αὐτὸν **νυκτός** ("He came to him **by night**"; John 3:2). The accusative of measure, in line with the basic function of the accusative as the limiting or defining case, commonly indicates the *extent* of time: ἀνετράφη **μῆνας τρεῖς** ἐν τῷ οἴκῳ τοῦ πατρός ("He [Moses] was raised **for three months** in his father's house"; Acts 7:20).

FEMININE

What It Looks Like

The majority of feminine nouns in Greek occur in the first declension, which means they have a stem ending in alpha or eta (α, η). Yet a noun's gender is not the same as its declension. A declension is a pattern of endings or "inflection" (for more on declension, see NOUN). While most first declension nouns are feminine, some are masculine (like ὁ μαθητής, "the disciple"). Similarly, while most second declension nouns (o stem) are masculine, some are feminine (like ἡ ὁδός, "the way"; see chart).

The following are some of the most common feminine noun endings:

Common Feminine Endings for Nouns

	1st Decl. η ending	1st Decl. α ending	1st Decl. α/η ending	2nd Decl. Fem.	3rd Decl. Fem.
Nom. Sg.	γραφή	ὥρα	δόξα	ὁδός	χάρις
Gen. Sg.	γραφῆς	ὥρας	δόξης	ὁδοῦ	χάριτος
Dat. Sg.	γραφῇ	ὥρᾳ	δόξῃ	ὁδῷ	χάριτι
Acc. Sg.	γραφήν	ὥραν	δόξαν	ὁδόν	χάριν
Nom. Pl.	γραφαί	ὧραι	δόξαι	ὁδοί	χάριτες
Gen. Pl.	γραφῶν	ὡρῶν	δοξῶν	ὁδῶν	χαρίτων
Dat. Pl.	γραφαῖς	ὥραις	δόξαις	ὁδοῖς	χάρισι(ν)
Acc. Pl.	γραφάς	ὥρας	δόξας	ὁδούς	χάριτας

What It Does

Gender refers to a classification assigned to nouns in many languages. In Greek every noun is classified as masculine, feminine, or neuter. (Hebrew has two genders—masculine and feminine.)

Grammatical gender is an arbitrary category and should not be confused with biological sex. While in Greek, terms for males are generally masculine and terms for females are generally feminine, the gender of most nouns has nothing to do with biological sex. Consider body parts: "head" (κεφαλή) is feminine; "mouth" (στόμα) is neuter; "eye" (ὀφθαλμός) is masculine; "tongue" (γλῶσσα) is feminine; "ear" (οὖς) is neuter; "neck" (τράχηλος) is masculine; "hand" is feminine (χείρ); "leg" (σκέλος) is neuter; "finger" (δάκτυλος) is masculine. Obviously, none of this has anything to do with biological gender. It might seem particularly odd that "breast" (μαστός) is masculine; the male reproductive organs, or "loins" (ὀσφῦς), are feminine, and the male "foreskin" (ἀκροβυστία) is feminine!

Nouns in Greek do not change their gender. For example, λόγος will always be masculine and γραφή will always be feminine. Adjectives, participles, and pronouns, by contrast, must be able to decline in all genders in order to agree with the gender of the noun they modify or the gender of their antecedent (= the word they refer back to). See ADJECTIVE; PARTICIPLE; PRONOUN, PERSONAL.

An Exegetical Insight

Gender identification can have significant exegetical and theological significance since a pronoun normally agrees with its antecedent (the word or phrase it refers back to) in number and gender. Consider, for example, Ephesians 2:8:

Τῇ γὰρ **χάριτί** ἐστε σεσῳσμένοι διὰ **πίστεως**· καὶ **τοῦτο** οὐκ ἐξ ὑμῶν, θεοῦ τὸ δῶρον·
"For **by grace** you have been saved through **faith**; and **this** is not from yourselves, it is a gift from God."

The antecedent to the demonstrative pronoun τοῦτο could be "grace" (χάρις) or "faith" (πίστις), or the entire preceding clause. Some commentators have claimed that it must be "faith," since this is the nearest antecedent. Faith itself, they argue, has its origin not in human will but as a gift from God. The problem, however, is that both χάρις and πίστις are feminine, while τοῦτο is neuter. While on very rare occasions an antecedent's gender may be different from the noun it refers to, a better explanation is that τοῦτο is referring here to neither "grace" nor "faith" individually, but "to the preceding clause as a whole, and thus to the whole process of salvation it describes, which of course includes faith as its means."[1] The whole of our salvation comes to us on the basis of God's gracious favor.

---

1. A. T. Lincoln, *Ephesians*, WBC 42 (Dallas: Word, 1990), 111–12.

FUTURE

What It Looks Like

The future tense is formed with a sigma (-σ) tense indicator, a connecting vowel, and the primary personal endings (the endings on present and future verbs). Its stem is based on the second principal part (see VERB). The future tense appears almost exclusively in the INDICATIVE mood, although there are a few future participles and future infinitives in the New Testament.

First Active Indicative (1st person plural; verb λύω)

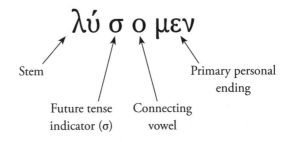

(verb: λύω)

Active			Middle			Passive		
Per. Sg.	Pl.		Per. Sg.	Pl.		Per. Sg.	Pl.	
1 λύ σ ω	λύ σ ο μεν		1 λύ σ ο μαι	λυ σ ό μεθα		1 λυ θή σ ο μαι	λυ θη σ ό μεθα	
2 λύ σ εις	λύ σ ε τε		2 λύ σ η	λύ σ ε σθε		2 λυ θή σ η	λυ θή σ ε σθε	
3 λύ σ ει	λύ σ ου σι(ν)		3 λύ σ ε ται	λύ σ ο νται		3 λυ θή σ ε ται	λυ θή σ ο νται	

What It Does

Tense in Greek can indicate both *time* of action (past, present, future) and *aspect*, or *kind* of action (see VERB). Only in the INDICATIVE mood do Greek verbs indicate time. Because the future tense occurs almost exclusively in the indicative, it generally indicates future action: "I will run." There are, however, various functions of the future that move beyond a simple future sense.

The most common functions of the future are the following:

1. *Predictive Future.* A future tense verb used to express an action that will take place in the future.

   μετὰ τρεῖς ἡμέρας **ἀναστήσεται**.
   "After three days **he will rise**." (Mark 9:31)

2. *Imperatival Future.* A future tense verb used to express a command.

> ἀγαπήσεις κύριον τὸν θεόν σου.
> "**[You shall] love** the Lord your God." (Matt 22:37)

3. *Deliberative Future.* A future tense verb used to ask a question that implies some doubt about the response.

> τί ἐροῦμεν; μὴ ἄδικος ὁ θεὸς . . . ;
> "What **shall we say?** Is God unjust . . . ?" (Rom 3:5)

An Exegetical Insight

Most examples of imperatival futures are quotations from the Old Testament, especially the legal material of the Pentateuch.[1] While this represents a literal rendering of the Hebrew, it also provides a more solemn tone than a simple imperative. Romans 13:9 reads οὐ μοιχεύσεις, οὐ φονεύσεις, οὐ κλέψεις, οὐκ ἐπιθυμήσεις ("you shall not commit adultery, you shall not murder, you shall not steal, you shall not covet"; citing Exod 20:13–17 and Deut 5:17–21; cf. also Matt 19:18). Contrary to what it might appear, using a future indicative instead of an imperative does not weaken the force of the imperative. It actually strengthens it.

---

1. Wallace, *Grammar*, 569.

GENITIVE

What It Looks Like

The genitive case is formed in the second declension (omicron stem; for declensions, see NOUN) with the connecting vowel followed by upsilon (-ου) and in the first declension (alpha or eta stem) with the connecting vowel followed by sigma (-ης or -ας). The third declension genitive singular ending is -ος. The plural ending is always -ων, whether in the first, second, or third declension.

λόγου

Stem   Connecting vowel   Case Ending

Genitive Forms Highlighted

	2ⁿᵈ Decl.	1ˢᵗ Decl.	2ⁿᵈ Decl. Neut.	3ʳᵈ Decl.	3ʳᵈ Decl. Neut.
Nom. Sg.	λόγος	γραφή	ἔργον	σάρξ	ὄνομα
Gen. Sg.	**λόγου**	**γραφῆς**	**ἔργου**	**σαρκός**	**ὀνόματος**
Dat. Sg.	λόγῳ	γραφῇ	ἔργῳ	σαρκί	ὀνόματι
Acc. Sg.	λόγον	γραφήν	ἔργον	σάρκα	ὄνομα
Nom. Pl.	λόγοι	γραφαί	ἔργα	σάρκες	ὀνόματα
Gen. Pl.	**λόγων**	**γραφῶν**	**ἔργων**	**σαρκῶν**	**ὀνομάτων**
Dat. Pl.	λόγοις	γραφαῖς	ἔργοις	σαρξί(ν)	ὀνόμασι(ν)
Acc. Pl.	λόγους	γραφάς	ἔργα	σάρκας	ὀνόματα

What It Does

The genitive case is one of five cases in Greek—NOMINATIVE, GENITIVE, DATIVE, ACCUSATIVE, and VOCATIVE. Case is the particular form of a noun or substantive that indicates its function. The genitive has the widest range of meanings among the Greek cases, with dozens of functions. Its most basic is *description*. The genitive is often translated with the prepositional phrase "of + NOUN" (e.g. "the word **of God**"), yet this rendering does not exhaust the diverse functions of the genitive. Here are a few of the most common:

1. *Attributive (or Descriptive) Genitive.* The genitive noun functions like an adjective modifying its head noun.

> τῷ ῥήματι **τῆς δυνάμεως** αὐτοῦ
> "by the word **of his power**" = "by his **powerful** word" (Heb 1:3)

2. *Possessive Genitive.* The head noun is owned by or belongs to the genitive noun or pronoun.

> Παῦλος δοῦλος **Χριστοῦ Ἰησοῦ.**
> "Paul a slave **of Christ Jesus**." (Rom 1:1)

3. *Genitive of Apposition.* The genitive noun or pronoun refers to the same thing as the noun it modifies, providing explanation or clarification. In this example, the temple *is* Jesus's body.

> ἔλεγεν περὶ τοῦ ναοῦ **τοῦ σώματος αὐτοῦ.**
> "He was speaking concerning the temple **of his body**." (John 2:21)

4. *Verbal Genitive (Subjective/Objective).* The genitive noun or pronoun functions either as the subject or the object of the head noun. The head noun always indicates a verbal idea.

> (1) Subjective: ἡ παρουσία **τοῦ υἱοῦ τοῦ ἀνθρώπου**
> "the coming **of the Son of Man**" (Matt 24:27)

> (2) Objective: ἡ **τοῦ πνεύματος** βλασφημία
> "the blasphemy **of the Spirit**" (Matt 12:31)

An Exegetical Insight

One of the most interesting proposed functions of the genitive in the New Testament is the "plenary" genitive, where the noun or pronoun in the genitive functions simultaneously as both a *subjective* and an *objective* genitive.[1] Consider Revelation 1:1: Ἀποκάλυψις **Ἰησοῦ Χριστοῦ** ("the revelation **of Jesus Christ**"). Does John mean that this is a revelation *from* Jesus (subjective genitive) or a revelation *about* Jesus Christ (objective genitive)? Or is it *both* (plenary genitive)? Similar is 2 Corinthians 5:14: ἡ γὰρ ἀγάπη **τοῦ Χριστοῦ** συνέχει ἡμᾶς ("For the love **of Christ** compels us"). Is this Christ's love for us (subjective), our love for Christ (objective), or both (plenary)? Some grammarians reject this category, while others affirm it as an intentional double meaning.

---

1. See Wallace, *Grammar*, 119–20, for the plausibility of this function.

IMPERATIVE

What It Looks Like

In English the imperative mood is formed by using the infinitive form of the verb without the word "to." So the imperative of "to go" is "Go!" The Greek imperative is formed with the verbal stem and the imperatival endings. The second person singular endings must be memorized, but the second plural is the same as the indicative form (-ετε). The third person singular (-ετω) and plural (-ετωσαν) endings must also be memorized. First aorist imperatives have the same endings except -σα replaces the epsilon (-ε) connecting vowel. Aorist imperatives do not have an augment, which occurs only in the indicative mood.

Present Active Imperative (2nd Singular; verb λύω)

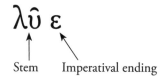

Stem   Imperatival ending

Main Imperatival Forms
Present and First Aorist (verb: λύω)

Per./Num.	Pres. Act.	Pres. Mid./Pass.	Aorist Act.	Aorist Mid.	Aorist Pass.
2nd Sg.	λῦε	λύου	λῦσον	λῦσαι	λύθητι
3rd Sg.	λυέτω	λυέσθω	λυσάτω	λυσάσθω	λυθήτω
2nd Pl.	λύετε	λύεσθε	λύσατε	λύσασθε	λύθητε
3rd Pl.	λυέτωσαν	λυέσθωσαν	λυσάτωσαν	λυσάσθωσαν	λυθήτωσαν

Second Aorist (verb: λείπω)

Per./Num.	2nd Aorist Act.	2nd Aorist Mid.	2nd Aorist Pass.
2nd Sg.	λίπε	λίπου	λίπητι
3rd Sg.	λιπέτω	λιπέσθω	λιπήτω
2nd Pl.	λίπετε	λίπεσθε	λίπητε
3rd Pl.	λιπέτωσαν	λιπέσθωσαν	λιπήτωσαν

What It Does

Mood is a feature of verbs that indicates the relationship between the verbal sense and reality. The imperative mood is the mood of intention or command. It indicates what the speaker would like to happen. The main functions of the imperative are command, request, prohibition, and permission.

1. *Command.*

   ὕπαγε ὀπίσω μου, σατανᾶ.
   "**Get** behind me, Satan!" (Mark 8:33)

2. *Request.* Often used when the speaker is addressing a superior.

   Καὶ εἶπαν οἱ ἀπόστολοι τῷ κυρίῳ· **πρόσθες** ἡμῖν πίστιν.
   "The apostles said to the Lord, '**Increase** our faith!'" (Luke 17:5)

3. *Prohibition.*

   μὴ συσχηματίζεσθε τῷ αἰῶνι τούτῳ.
   "**Do not be conformed** to this age." (Rom 12:2)

4. *Permission.*

   τὸ νῦν ἔχον **πορεύου.**
   "**You may leave** for now." (Acts 24:25)

An Exegetical Insight

Although the imperative is often called the mood of *command*, the examples above show that it is much more than that. Although it always expresses the intention of the speaker, it is by no means always a forceful or authoritative command. Indeed, at times we could call it the mood of encouragement. Jesus teaches his disciples that their heavenly Father knows when the smallest sparrow falls to earth, "So **don't be afraid**, you are worth more that many sparrows!" (**μὴ** οὖν **φοβεῖσθε**· πολλῶν στρουθίων διαφέρετε ὑμεῖς; Matt 10:31). When the disciples are terrified when Jesus approaches them walking on water, he assures them, "**Take courage!** It is I. **Don't be afraid**" (**θαρσεῖτε**, ἐγώ εἰμι· **μὴ φοβεῖσθε**; Mark 6:50). When the women are shocked to discover the empty tomb, an angel assures them, "**Don't be alarmed**; you are seeking Jesus of Nazareth who was crucified. He is risen! He is not here" (**μὴ ἐκθαμβεῖσθε**· Ἰησοῦν ζητεῖτε τὸν Ναζαρηνὸν τὸν ἐσταυρωμένον· ἠγέρθη, οὐκ ἔστιν ὧδε; Mark 16:6). These "commands" are actually great words of encouragement—for them and for us.

IMPERFECT

What It Looks Like

The imperfect tense is built on the present tense stem (the first principal part; see VERB) with an epsilon augment (ε-) at the beginning of the verb, a connecting vowel, and the secondary personal endings (the endings on aorist, imperfect, and perfect verbs). The imperfect occurs only in the INDICATIVE mood.

Imperfect Active Indicative (1st person singular; verb: λύω)

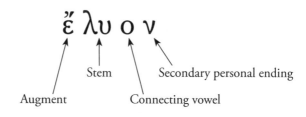

Imperfect Indicative Paradigm (verb: λύω)

Active			Middle/Passive		
Per. Sg.		Pl.	Per. Sg.		Pl.
1ˢᵗ ἔ λυ ον		ἐ λύ ομεν	1ˢᵗ ἐ λυ ό μην		ἐ λυ ό μεθα
2ⁿᵈ ἔ λυ ε ς		ἐ λύ ετε	2ⁿᵈ ἐ λύ ου		ἐ λύ ε σθε
3ʳᵈ ἔ λυ ε(ν)		ἔ λυ ον	3ʳᵈ ἐ λύ ε το		ἐ λύ ο ντο

What It Does

Tense in Greek can indicate the *time* of an action as well as *aspect*, or kind of action (see VERB). Aspect, however, is always primary. Only in the indicative does time become a factor. The time of action for the imperfect is past time. The aspect, like the PRESENT tense, is *imperfective,* continuous or progressive ("he was running"). This contrasts with the AORIST, which indicates simple or perfective past time, meaning action viewed as a whole or in summary ("he ran"). It is sometimes said that while the aorist tense takes a snapshot of the action, the imperfect takes a motion picture, portraying the action as it unfolds.[1]

There are various functions of imperfects, though all in some sense portray the action as ongoing. Here are the main ones:

---

1. See Wallace, *Grammar*, 541.

1. *Progressive Imperfect.* Describes an action or state that was in progress in the past.

   > τί ἐν τῇ ὁδῷ **διελογίζεσθε**;
   > "What **were you arguing** about on the road?" (Mark 9:33)

2. *Ingressive Imperfect.* Stresses the beginning of the action, often translated, "began . . ."

   > **ἐδίδασκεν** αὐτοὺς . . .
   > "He **began teaching** them . . ." (Matt 5:2)

3. *Iterative Imperfect.* Expresses the repeated nature of an action.

   > **ἤρχετο** πρὸς αὐτόν.
   > "She **kept coming** to him." (Luke 18:3)

4. *Customary Imperfect.* Stresses the recurring or habitual nature of an action. It is similar to an *iterative* imperfect, except that the customary indicates something that is regular and periodic, while the iterative indicates something merely repeated.

   > **ἐπορεύοντο** οἱ γονεῖς αὐτοῦ κατ᾽ ἔτος εἰς Ἰερουσαλήμ.
   > "His parents **used to go** to Jerusalem each year." (Luke 2:41)

5. *Conative Imperfect.* Also called the *tendential* or *voluntative imperfect.* Emphasizes an ongoing attempt or desire.

   > ἐδίωκον τὴν ἐκκλησίαν τοῦ θεοῦ καὶ **ἐπόρθουν** αὐτήν.
   > "I persecuted the church of God and **tried to destroy** it." (Gal 1:13)

An Exegetical Insight

The IMPERFECT tense appears frequently in narrative since stories are usually told in the past tense and have a progressive or ongoing nature about them.

The difference between the imperfect and the aorist is evident in the use of the verb λέγω ("say"). While the aorist (εἶπεν; "he said") tends to be used "for a simple reference to an utterance previously made," the imperfect (ἔλεγεν) is commonly used "for the delineation of the content of a speech."[2] Longer discourses, like the sermon beginning in Luke 6:20, tend to be introduced with the imperfect.

---

2. BDF, 170 (§329).

INDICATIVE

What It Looks Like

The forms of the indicative mood are too numerous to list here; only the present indicative is shown. For the indicative mood of other tenses, see the entries for FUTURE, IMPERFECT, AORIST, PERFECT, and PLUPERFECT.

Present Indicative Paradigm (verb: λύω)

Active			Middle/Passive		
Per.	Sg.	Pl.	Per.	Sg.	Pl.
1st	λύ ω	λύ ο μεν	1st	λύ ο μαι	λυ ό μεθα
2nd	λύ εις	λύ ε τε	2nd	λύ η	λύ ε σθε
3rd	λύ ει	λύ ου σι(ν)	3rd	λύ ε ται	λύ ο νται

What It Does

Mood is a feature of verbs that indicates the relationship between the verbal sense and reality. The indicative mood is the mood of reality. It indicates *real* action. (*Example:* "He ran."). Contrast this with the SUBJUNCTIVE mood, the mood of potentiality (*Example:* "He might run.").

1. *Declarative Indicative.* An indicative used to make a statement.

   ἐπ᾽ ἐσχάτου τῶν ἡμερῶν τούτων **ἐλάλησεν** ἡμῖν ἐν υἱῷ.
   "In these last days **he has spoken** to us by his Son." (Heb 1:2)

   τὸ δοκίμιον ὑμῶν τῆς πίστεως **κατεργάζεται** ὑπομονήν.
   "The testing of your faith **produces** endurance." (Jas 1:3)

2. *Interrogative Indicative.* An indicative used to ask a question.

   σὺ **εἶ** ὁ βασιλεὺς τῶν Ἰουδαίων;
   "**Are you** the king of the Jews?" (Mark 15:2)

   τί **ποιήσωμεν** τοῖς ἀνθρώποις τούτοις;
   "What **shall we do** with these men?" (Acts 4:16)

3. *Potential Indicative.* An indicative expressing potential action, whether a wish, an obligation, a command, or a condition. This use overlaps with other moods (See SUBJUNCTIVE, OPTATIVE, IMPERATIVE).

- *Wish or Desire* (with verbs of wishing or desire)

  Οὐ γὰρ **θέλω** ὑμᾶς ἀγνοεῖν, ἀδελφοί . . .
  "For **I** do not **want** you to be unaware, brothers and sisters . . ." (Rom 11:25)

- *Obligation* (with verbs of obligation or necessity)

  ἐν Ἱεροσολύμοις ἐστὶν ὁ τόπος ὅπου προσκυνεῖν **δεῖ**.
  "Jerusalem is the place where **it is necessary** to worship." (John 4:20)

  Ἀνὴρ . . . οὐκ **ὀφείλει** κατακαλύπτεσθαι τὴν κεφαλὴν.
  "A man . . . **ought** not to cover his head." (1 Cor 11:7)

- *Command* (with the future indicative [imperatival future])

  ἅγιοι **ἔσεσθε**, ὅτι ἐγὼ ἅγιος.
  "**Be** holy, because I am holy." (1 Pet 1:16; quoting Lev 11:44)

- *Condition* (the indicative used in first or second class conditions, where the protasis is in the indicative; see CONJUNCTION, CONDITIONAL)

  εἰ υἱὸς **εἶ** τοῦ θεοῦ, βάλε σεαυτὸν ἐντεῦθεν κάτω.
  "**If you are** the Son of God, throw yourself down from here." (Luke 4:9)

An Exegetical Insight

It is important to recognize that the reality or actuality of the indicative is *from the perspective of the speaker.* For example, the statement, "He is a liar," may not be true, but the speaker is expressing it as though it were.

In Mark 2, when the teachers of the law hear Jesus pronounce forgiveness of sins for the paralyzed man, they reply, "He's blaspheming! Who can forgive sins but God alone?" (Mark 2:7). The verb "he blasphemes" (βλασφημεῖ) is in the indicative, not because the statement is true, but because it is true from the perspective of the speakers. They are declaring Jesus to be blaspheming. Of course in what follows Jesus proves, by healing the man, that he is not blaspheming, since "the Son of Man has authority on earth to forgive sins" (Mark 2:10).

INFINITIVE

What It Looks Like

In English the infinitive is formed by adding "to" to the basic or lexical form of the verb: "to go," "to eat," "to run." Most infinitives in Greek end in either -ειν or -αι (see chart below).

Infinitive Forms (verbs: λύω; λαμβάνω; γράφω)

Present Active λύειν	First Aorist Active λῦσαι	Second Aorist Active λαβεῖν (verb: λαμβάνω)	Perfect Active λελυκέναι
Present Middle λύεσθαι	First Aorist Middle λύσασθαι	Second Aorist Middle λαβέσθαι (verb: λαμβάνω)	Perfect Middle λελύσθαι
Present Passive λύεσθαι	First Aorist Passive λυθῆναι	Second Aorist Passive γραφῆναι (verb: γράφω)	Perfect Passive λελύσθαι

What It Does

The infinitive is a verbal noun. Although often identified as a Greek mood, the infinitive is actually a *verbal,* a word derived from a verb that functions as another part of speech (in this case, a noun with verbal characteristics).

Infinitives can function substantivally (as a noun) or adverbially (modifying a verb):

1. *Substantival.*

   - As a nominative *subject.*

     τὰ αὐτὰ **γράφειν** ὑμῖν ἐμοὶ μὲν οὐκ ὀκνηρόν.
     "**To write** the same things to you is no bother for me." (Phil 3:1)

   - As an accusative *object.*

     οὐ παραιτοῦμαι **τὸ ἀποθανεῖν**.
     "I do not refuse **to face death**." (Acts 25:11)

   - As the *object* of a preposition (see examples below).

2. *Adverbial.*

   - *Purpose.* Modifying a verb in terms of purpose (occurs with the infinitive alone; τοῦ + inf.; εἰς τό + inf.; πρὸς τό + inf.).

     ἔπεμψα **εἰς τὸ γνῶναι** τὴν πίστιν ὑμῶν.
     "I sent **in order to know about** your faith." (1 Thess 3:5)

- *Result.* Modifying a verb in terms of result (occurs with the infinitive alone; τοῦ + inf.; ὥστε + inf.; εἰς τό + inf.).

  οὐδεὶς ἐπιθήσεταί σοι **τοῦ κακῶσαί** σε.
  "No one will attack you **with the result to harm** you." (Acts 18:10)

- *Temporal.* Identifying the time at which a verbal action occurred (occurs with πρὸ τοῦ + inf. ["before"]; ἐν τῷ + inf. ["while"]; μετὰ τό + inf. ["after"]).

  πρὸ τοῦ σε Φίλιππον **φωνῆσαι** . . . εἶδόν σε.
  "**Before** Philip **called** you . . . I saw you." (John 1:48)

- *Causal.* Expressing the cause or reason for a verbal action (occurs with the infinitive alone; διὰ τό + inf.).

  οὐκ ἔχετε **διὰ τὸ μὴ αἰτεῖσθαι** ὑμᾶς.
  "You do not have, **because** you **do not ask**." (Jas 4:2)

- *Complementary.* Completing the action of certain verbs.

  σῴζειν . . . **δύναται** τοὺς προσερχομένους.
  "**He is able . . . to save** those who draw near." (Heb 7:25)

An Exegetical Insight

Infinitives are built from a verbal root and have tense and voice, but function as nouns. This concept is well illustrated in one of Paul's most famous statements, Philippians 1:21:

Ἐμοὶ γὰρ **τὸ ζῆν** Χριστὸς καὶ **τὸ ἀποθανεῖν** κέρδος.
"For to me, **to live** is Christ and **to die** is gain."

The infinitives ζῆν ("to live"; from ζάω) and ἀποθανεῖν ("to die"; from ἀποθνῄσκω) are functioning as the subjects of their respective clauses. The neuter article (τό) emphasizes this substantival function. The verb "is" is implied and the nouns "Christ" and "gain" are predicate nominatives. Paul's whole life, he says, is focused and centered on Christ, so that he can say, "To live *is* Christ."

INTERJECTION

What It Looks Like

Interjections do not change their form (inflect). The following are interjections that appear in the New Testament:

Interjection	Translation	Frequency
ἰδού	*Behold! Look! See! Listen!*	200
οὐαί	*Woe! Alas! How terrible for you!*	46
ἴδε	*Behold! Look! See! Listen!*	28
ὦ	*O! You!*	17
δεῦτε	*Come!*	12
δεῦρο	*Come! Come here!*	8
ἄγε	*Come! Go!*	2
ἔα	*Hey! Ah! Alas! Go away!*	1

What It Does

An interjection or exclamation is a word used to express an emotional response. In English words like "Oh!" "Aha!" "Yum!" and "Yay!" are interjections. Interjections are relatively rare in the New Testament

Examples:

ἰδοὺ ἀποστέλλω τὸν ἄγγελόν μου πρὸ προσώπου σου.
"**Look!** I am sending my messenger ahead of you." (Luke 7:27)

οὐαί σοι, Χοραζίν, **οὐαί** σοι, Βηθσαϊδά.
"**Woe** to you Chorazin! **Woe** to you, Bethsaida!" (Matt 11:21)

ἴδε νῦν ἠκούσατε τὴν βλασφημίαν.
"**Look**, now you have heard the blasphemy!" (Matt 26:65)

ὦ ἀνόητοι καὶ βραδεῖς τῇ καρδίᾳ τοῦ πιστεύειν ἐπὶ πᾶσιν οἷς ἐλάλησαν οἱ προφῆται.
"**O** foolish ones and slow of heart to believe in all that the prophets spoke!" (Luke 24:25)

ἔα, τί ἡμῖν καὶ σοί, Ἰησοῦ Ναζαρηνέ;
"**Ah!** What do want with us, Jesus of Nazareth?" (Luke 4:34)

An Exegetical Insight

Greek exclamations or interjections can be tricky to translate. This is because Greek exclamations often differ from those in English in sound, meaning, and function. For example, the Greek exclamations ἰδού and ἴδε are likely formed from imperative forms of εἶδον ("I saw"), and so English versions commonly translate them with a verb of seeing: "Behold!" or "Look!" Yet "behold" is archaic English, seldom used today, and "look" sounds very unnatural in most contexts where ἰδού appears. Consider Matthew 2:19 NASB: "But when Herod died, behold [ἰδού], an angel of the Lord appeared in a dream to Joseph in Egypt, and said . . ." Is the reader here being told to look, and if so, where? The word ἰδού is used here to announce a startling or supernatural event and means something like, "Wow, this is amazing!" Does "behold" convey this sense?

Another exclamation that is archaic and not common English today is ὦ ("O!"), which appears seventeen times in the New Testament. The more formal equivalent (or "literal") versions tend to translate it as "O" as in Matthew 15:28 NASB: "Then Jesus said to her, 'O woman, your faith is great!'" Yet in English, we don't speak this way (unless we're trying to sound "biblical"). Readers will likely mistake it for the English exclamation "Oh!" a different word that indicates surprise. Some versions therefore translate the word as "you," as in Matthew 17:17 NIV ("You [ὦ] unbelieving and perverse generation") or simply leave it untranslated, allowing the context to carry over the meaning (see NIV and NLT in Matt 15:28; Luke 24:25; Acts 1:1; 13:10; 18:14; etc.).

Consider also the exclamation used by the demon in Luke 4:34: ἔα, τί ἡμῖν καὶ σοί, Ἰησοῦ Ναζαρηνέ; ("**Ea!** What do want with us, Jesus of Nazareth?"; Luke 4:34). Does the translator simply transliterate the Greek word as *Ea!,* or do they try to find an English equivalent? Here is what various versions do: "Ha!" (NET; NAB; NJB; ESV); "Hey!" (CEB; CEV); "Oh, no!" (GW); "Go away!" (NIV); "Leave us alone!" (HCSB; cf. NRSV; NKJV).

Translators will continue to wrestle with how best to translate exclamations, since they seldom have direct parallels in English.

MASCULINE

What It Looks Like

The majority of masculine nouns in Greek occur in the second declension, which means they have a stem ending (also called a connecting vowel) in omicron (o), sometimes lengthened to omega (ω). Yet a noun's gender is not the same as its declension. A declension is a pattern of endings or "inflection" (for more on declension, see NOUN). While most second declension nouns (o stem) are masculine, some are feminine (like ἡ ὁδός, "the way"). Similarly, while most first declension nouns (α or η stem) are feminine, some are masculine (like ὁ προφήτης, "the prophet"; see chart below).

The following are common masculine noun endings:

Some Masculine Noun Endings in 1ˢᵗ, 2ⁿᵈ, and 3ʳᵈ Declensions

Case/Num.	2ⁿᵈ Decl. Masc.	1ˢᵗ Decl. Masc.	3ʳᵈ Decl. Masc.	3ʳᵈ Decl. Masc.
Nom. Sg.	λόγος	προφήτης	ἀνήρ	βασιλεύς
Gen. Sg.	λόγου	προφήτου	ἀνδρός	βασιλέως
Dat. Sg.	λόγῳ	προφήτῃ	ἀνδρί	βασιλεῖ
Acc. Sg.	λόγον	προφήτην	ἄνδρα	βασιλέα
Nom. Pl.	λόγοι	προφῆται	ἄνδρες	βασιλεῖς
Gen. Pl.	λόγων	προφητῶν	ἀνδρῶν	βασιλέων
Dat. Pl.	λόγοις	προφήταις	ἀνδράσι(ν)	βασιλεῦσι(ν)
Acc. Pl.	λόγους	προφήτας	ἄνδρας	βασιλεῖς

What It Does

Gender refers to a classification assigned to nouns in many languages. In Greek every noun is classified as masculine, feminine, or neuter. (Hebrew has two genders, masculine and feminine.) Grammatical gender is an arbitrary category and should not be confused with biological sex. While in Greek, terms for males are generally masculine and terms for females are generally feminine, the gender of most nouns has nothing to do with biological sex. A word meaning "sword" (μάχαιρα) in Greek, for example, is feminine, while a word meaning "shield" is masculine (θυρεός). Synonyms can be different genders. θυμός (masculine) and ὀργή (feminine) both can mean "anger," "wrath," or "fury." Similarly, οἰκία (feminine) and οἶκος (masculine) both mean "house" or "home." Their gender is purely a grammatical category.

Nouns in Greek do not change their gender. For example, λόγος will always be masculine and γραφή will always be feminine. Adjectives, participles, and pronouns, by contrast, must be able to decline in all genders in order to agree with the gender of the noun they modify or the gender of their antecedent (= the word they refer back to). (See ADJECTIVE; PARTICIPLE; PRONOUN, PERSONAL.)

Greek, like many other languages, uses the masculine gender as the default or generic gender. For example, ἄνθρωποι (masculine plural) often means "people" and is used when both men and women are present. ἀδελφοί (masculine plural) can mean either "brothers" or "brothers and sisters" depending on the context, whereas ἀδελφαί (feminine plural) would mean only "sisters." Similarly, the masculine plural pronoun (αὐτοί; "they") is used when only men or when both men and women are being referred to, whereas the feminine plural pronoun (αὐταί) would be used for a group of women.

An Exegetical Insight

Since English does not distinguish nouns according to grammatical gender, there is a tendency for English language students to wrongly impose biological gender on what is a grammatical category.

For example, it is sometimes said that ἄνθρωπος *literally* means "man" or that ἀδελφοί *literally* means "brothers" because these are masculine terms. This misunderstands both the nature of word meanings (lexical semantics) as well as the function of gender. ἄνθρωπος does not have a "literal" meaning. It has a range of possible senses, and these include *man, person, human being, mankind, humanity*, etc.[1] It is the context that determines which sense is intended. Similarly, ἀδελφοί has a range of meanings, including *brothers, siblings, brothers and sisters, fellow members* (of a group), *fellow Christians*, etc. It is the context that determines which sense is intended. The masculine gender in these cases is grammatical, not biological.

---

1. BDAG, 81–82.

MIDDLE

What It Looks Like

Since the middle voice is a feature of all the verbal moods (INDICATIVE, SUBJUNCTIVE, IMPERATIVE, OPTATIVE) and verbals (PARTICIPLE, INFINITIVE), there are a great many forms the middle voice can take. The following are the middle forms in the INDICATIVE mood. For middle forms in other moods and verbals, see their particular entries.

Middle Indicative in Various Tenses (verbs: λύω; λείπω)

Present Middle/Passive		Future Middle		Imperfect Middle/Passive	
Per. Sg.	Pl.	Pers. Sg.	Pl.	Pers. Sg.	Pl.
1st λύ ο μαι	λυ ό μεθα	1st λύ σ ο μαι	λυ σ ό μεθα	1st ἐ λυ ό μην	ἐ λυ ο μεθα
2nd λύ ῃ	λύ ε σθε	2nd λύ σ ῃ	λύ σ ε σθε	2nd ἐ λύ ου	ἐ λύ ε σθε
3rd λύ ε ται	λύ ο νται	3rd λύ σ ε ται	λύ σ ο νται	3rd ἐ λύ ε το	ἐ λύ ο ντο

Perfect Middle/Passive		Pluperfect Middle/Passive		1st Aorist Middle	
Per. Sg.	Pl.	Pers. Sg.	Pl.	Pers. Sg.	Pl.
1st λέ λυ μαι	λε λύ μεθα	1st ἐ λε λύ μην	ἐ λε λύ μεθα	1st ἐλυ σά μην	ἐ λυ σ ά μεθα
2nd λέ λυ σαι	λέ λυ σθε	2nd ἐ λέ λυ σο	ἐ λέ λυ σθε	2nd ἐ λύ σ ω	ἐ λύ σ α σθε
3rd λέ λυ ται	λέ λυ νται	3rd ἐ λέ λυ το	ἐ λέ λυ ντο	3rd ἐ λύ σ α το	ἐ λύ σ α ντο

				2nd Aorist Middle (irregular stem)	
				Pers. Sg.	Pl.
				1st ἐ λιπ ό μην	ἐ λιπ ό μεθα
				2nd ἐ λίπ ου	ἐ λίπ ε σθε
				3rd ἐ λίπ ε το	ἐ λίπ ο ντο

What It Does

Voice indicates the relationship of the subject of a sentence to its verb, whether it is *acting* or *being acted upon*. The middle voice is one of three Greek voices: ACTIVE, MIDDLE, and PASSIVE. In the middle, the subject is in some sense both acting *and* participating in the action. It is hard for English speakers to comprehend the middle, since we do not have it in English. Perhaps the closest we have is a reflexive construction, where the agent both acts and is acted upon: "He shaved (himself)" (see *direct or reflexive middle*, below). The following are the most common functions of the middle voice in the New Testament:

1. *Deponent middles* are by far the most common middles in the NT. Deponent means active in meaning but middle in form. Examples

of deponent verbs in the NT are ἔρχομαι ("I come"); δύναμαι ("I am able"); πορεύομαι ("I go"). It should be noted that many scholars view deponency as an artificial category for non-Greek speakers. The Greeks likely thought of these verbs as true middles (in some sense), but we hear them as active in English since we do not have a middle voice.

2. *Direct or Reflexive Middle.* The subject acts on itself.

> ἀπήγξατο.
> "He [Judas] **hanged himself**." (Matt 27:5)

> τίς **παρασκευάσεται** εἰς πόλεμον;
> Who **will prepare themselves** for battle?" (1 Cor 14:8)

3. *Indirect or Intensive Middle.* The subject acts for itself or for its own benefit.

> Μαριὰμ γὰρ τὴν ἀγαθὴν μερίδα **ἐξελέξατο.**
> "Mary **has chosen [for herself]** the best part." (Luke 10:42)

Other rare types include permissive, causative, and reciprocal middles.

An Exegetical Insight

One debated middle appears in 1 Corinthians 13:8:

εἴτε γλῶσσαι, **παύσονται.**
"If there are tongues, **they will cease**."

Some have argued that the middle voice here indicates that tongues will "cease by themselves" or will gradually die out (an *indirect middle*). This, then, is sometimes linked to the view that tongues ceased during the first century, after the apostles passed from the scene. Other interpreters reject this view by claiming that the verb παύω is deponent in the future tense and so means simply "they will cease," not "they will cease by themselves." There is little difference, however, in translating the clause as "they will cease" or "they will cease by themselves." Both simply mean they *themselves* will stop. In any case, Paul does not link the cessation of these gifts to the death of the apostles. Rather, the cessation of tongues and other sign gifts is connected with the coming of τὸ τέλειον ("the perfect," "perfection," or "completion"; 1 Cor 13:10), which is almost certainly a reference to the second coming of Christ, when we shall see him "face to face" and "shall know fully," even as we are "fully known" (1 Cor 13:12).

NEUTER

What It Looks Like

Neuter nouns decline in the second or third declension (for more on declensions, see NOUN). The second declension refers to nouns with stems ending in omicron (o). The third declension refers to stems ending in a consonant. Neuter nouns always have the same form in the nominative and accusative. Neuter plural nouns almost always end in alpha (α) in the nominative and accusative. The dative and genitive endings of neuter nouns are the same as their masculine counterparts. Representative paradigms in the second and third declension are shown below:

Some Neuter Nouns in 2nd and 3rd Declensions

Case/Num.	2nd Declension Neuter	3rd Declension Neuter	3rd Declension Neuter (-ματ)
Nom. Sg.	ἔργον	φῶς	ὄνομα
Gen. Sg.	ἔργου	φωτός	ὀνόματος
Dat. Sg.	ἔργῳ	φωτί	ὀνόματι
Acc. Sg.	ἔργον	φῶς	ὄνομα
Nom. Pl.	ἔργα	φῶτα	ὀνόματα
Gen. Pl.	ἔργων	φώτων	ὀνομάτων
Dat. Pl.	ἔργοις	φώσι(ν)	ὀνόμασι(ν)
Acc. Pl.	ἔργα	φῶτα	ὀνόματα

What It Does

Gender refers to a classification assigned to nouns. In Greek every noun is classified as masculine, feminine, or neuter. Grammatical gender is an arbitrary category and should not be confused with biological gender. While in Greek, terms for males are generally masculine and terms for females are generally feminine, the gender of most nouns has nothing to do with biological sex. Some words for children are neuter (τέκνον ["child"]; τεκνίον ["little child"]; παιδίον ["little child"]; κοράσιον ["girl"]); others are masculine (παῖς ["child" or "servant"]; υἱός ["son" or "child"]); and still others are feminine (θυγάτηρ, "daughter").

The word for "spirit" (πνεῦμα) used for the Holy Spirit is neuter, even though the Spirit is a person, not a thing. In Hebrew, the word for "spirit" (רוּחַ, *ruakh*) is usually feminine. This does not mean the Spirit is female (or male). This is grammatical, not biological, gender.

Nouns in Greek do not change their gender. For example, ἔργον will always be neuter, λόγος will always be masculine, and γραφή will always be feminine. Adjectives, participles, and pronouns, by contrast, must be able to decline in all genders in order to agree with the gender of the noun they modify or the gender of their antecedent (= the word they refer back to). See ADJECTIVE; PARTICIPLE; PRONOUN, PERSONAL.

One important idiom to be aware of is that neuter plural nouns in Greek commonly take singular verbs. Here are some examples:

καὶ ... **τὰ κυνάρια** [pl.] **ἐσθίει** [sg.] ἀπὸ τῶν ψιχίων τῶν πιπτόντων ἀπὸ τῆς τραπέζης τῶν κυρίων αὐτῶν.
"Even **the dogs eat** the crumbs that fall from their master's table." (Matt 15:27)

οὐκ οἴδατε ὅτι **τὰ σώματα** [pl.] ὑμῶν μέλη Χριστοῦ **ἐστιν** [sg.];
"Do you not know that your **bodies are** members of Christ?" (1 Cor 6:15)

An Exegetical Insight

As noted above, a neuter noun does not necessarily mean that the reference is to a thing rather than a person. As we mentioned earlier, common words for children are neuter in Greek (τέκνον; τεκνίον; παιδίον). It's not that the ancients viewed little children as sexless; after all, terms like τέκνον are often used of adult "children." Throughout 1–3 John, the author refers to believers as "little children" (τεκνία; 1 John 2:1, 12, 28; 3:18; 4:4; 5:21) and "children" (τέκνα; 1 John 3:1, 2, 10; 5:2; 2 John 1, 4, 13; 3 John 4). These are clearly metaphorical references, identifying them as part of the family of God. The neuter gender of τεκνία and τέκνα is purely grammatical.

It is a debated point whether masculine pronouns are ever used with reference to the Holy Spirit to emphasize his personhood. While in most cases neuter pronouns are used, a possible exception appears in John 16:13:

ὅταν δὲ ἔλθῃ **ἐκεῖνος, τὸ πνεῦμα** τῆς ἀληθείας
"But when **that one, the Spirit** of truth, comes . . ." (John 16:13)

Here the masculine pronoun ἐκεῖνος is used with reference to the Spirit, perhaps to identify him as a person. A simpler explanation, however, is that the masculine pronoun is referring back to the masculine antecedent ὁ παράκλητος ("the Advocate") in 16:7. A similar example can be found in John 14:26. Evidence for the personhood of the Holy Spirit is better demonstrated through actions and attributes given to him (such as teaching, testifying, guiding, convicting, etc.) rather than through a gender designation that is grammatical rather than biological.

NOMINATIVE

What It Looks Like

The nominative case is the most easily recognizable of the Greek cases, since it is the lexical or default form of the noun (the one you look up in a lexicon). Second declension (for declension, see NOUN) singular nouns have an omicron connecting vowel (o) followed by a sigma (ς) as their case ending. First declension nouns have no ending except their alpha (α) or eta (η) connecting vowel. The nominative plural endings are the connecting vowel followed by iota (-οι, -αι) in the second and first declensions and epsilon sigma (-ες) in the third declension. Third declension singular nouns either end in sigma (-ς) or have no ending. Neuter nouns and adjectives always have the same form in the nominative and accusative; the neuter plural nominative and accusative nouns end in alpha (-α) in all declensions.

Stem   Connecting vowel   Case Ending

Nominative Forms Highlighted

Case/Num.	2nd Decl.	1st Decl.	2nd Decl. Neut.	3rd Decl.	3rd Decl. Neut.
Nom. Sg.	λόγος	γραφή	ἔργον	σάρξ	ὄνομα
Gen. Sg.	λόγου	γραφῆς	ἔργου	σαρκός	ὀνόματος
Dat. Sg.	λόγῳ	γραφῇ	ἔργῳ	σαρκί	ὀνόματι
Acc. Sg.	λόγον	γραφήν	ἔργον	σάρκα	ὄνομα
Nom. Pl.	λόγοι	γραφαί	ἔργα	σάρκες	ὀνόματα
Gen. Pl.	λόγων	γραφῶν	ἔργων	σαρκῶν	ὀνομάτων
Dat. Pl.	λόγοις	γραφαῖς	ἔργοις	σαρξί(ν)	ὀνόμασι(ν)
Acc. Pl.	λόγους	γραφάς	ἔργα	σάρκας	ὀνόματα

What It Does

The nominative case is one of five cases in Greek—NOMINATIVE, GENITIVE, DATIVE, ACCUSATIVE, and VOCATIVE. The basic function of the nominative case is to name or designate something. The following are some of its main functions:

1. *Subject.* The most common use of the nominative is as the subject of a sentence.

> ἠγάπησεν **ὁ θεὸς** τὸν κόσμον.
> "**God** loved the world." (John 3:16)

2. *Predicate nominative* is a noun, pronoun, or other substantive in the nominative case that is equated in some sense with the subject and is connected to it with an equative (or copulative) verb. The most common equative verbs are εἰμί, γίνομαι, and ὑπάρχω.

> ἐγώ εἰμι **ὁ ἄρτος** τῆς ζωῆς.
> "I am **the bread** of life." (John 6:35)

3. *Nominative Pendens.* A pendant (or "hanging") nominative is a word or phrase that is grammatically independent of the rest of the sentence.

> **Ὁ νικῶν** ποιήσω αὐτὸν στῦλον.
> "**The one who overcomes**—I will make him to be a pillar." (Rev 3:12)

4. *Nominative Absolute.* Similar to a nominative pendens, but here the independent nominative appears in introductory material, such as a title, heading, greeting, or address.

> **Ἀρχὴ** τοῦ εὐαγγελίου Ἰησοῦ Χριστοῦ.
> "**The beginning** of the gospel of Jesus Christ." (Mark 1:1)

An Exegetical Insight

Note these curious nominatives in Revelation 1:4:

χάρις ὑμῖν καὶ εἰρήνη ἀπὸ **ὁ ὢν** καὶ **ὁ ἦν** καὶ **ὁ ἐρχόμενος**.
"Grace and peace to you from '**the One Who Is**' and '**the One Who Was**' and '**the Coming One**.'" (Rev 1:4)

The grammar throughout Revelation is unusual, but this is perhaps the strangest of all. The preposition ἀπό should normally take its object in the genitive case, but instead here it takes three *nominative* objects. Yet John is using this "bad" grammar to make a powerful point. By using the article and the nominative case instead of the genitive, he highlights these three phrases as exalted titles. This emphasizes the central theme of Revelation: *God is the sovereign Lord of history.* He is in charge of the present (ὁ ὢν), the past (ὁ ἦν) and the future (ὁ ἐρχόμενος). God launched human history and he will bring it to its determined end. He is Lord of all.

NOUN

What It Looks Like

Nouns in Greek follow three *declensions,* or patterns. First declension nouns have stems ending in alpha (α) or eta (η). (This stem ending may also be called a connecting vowel.) Second declension nouns have stems ending in omicron (o), which sometimes lengthens to an omega (ω). Third declension nouns have stems ending in consonants, which often collide with other consonants and change their form (e.g., σαρκ + ς = σάρξ).

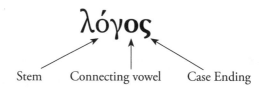

Stem   Connecting vowel   Case Ending

Noun Declension Endings (with connecting vowel)

Case/Num.	2nd Decl. (o) Masc.	1st Decl. (α/η) Fem.	2nd Decl. (o) Neut.	3rd Decl. Masc./Fem.	3rd Decl. Neut.
Nom. Sg.	-ος	-η, -α	-ον	-ς, —	—
Gen. Sg.	-ου	-ης, -ας	-ου	-ος	-ος
Dat. Sg.	-ῳ	-ῃ, -ᾳ	-ῳ	-ι	-ι
Acc. Sg.	-ον	-ην, -αν	-ον	-α, -ν	—
Nom. Pl.	-οι	-αι	-α	-ες	-α
Gen. Pl.	-ων	-ων	-ων	-ων	-ων
Dat. Pl.	-οις	-αις	-οις	-σι(ν)	-σι(ν)
Acc. Pl.	-ους	-ας	-α	-ας	-α

Most first declension nouns are feminine. Most second declension nouns are masculine or neuter. Examples of exceptions are first declension masculine nouns like ὁ μαθητής ("the disciple") and second declension feminine nouns like ἡ ὁδός ("the way").

What It Does

Nouns are words that designate persons, places, things, or ideas. Greek nouns are categorized by *case*, *gender*, and *number*.

1. *Case.* Case is the particular form of the noun that indicates its function in the sentence. There are five cases in Greek. For more details, see NOMINATIVE, GENITIVE, DATIVE, ACCUSATIVE, VOCATIVE.

2. *Gender.* In Greek every noun has grammatical gender, masculine, feminine, or neuter. Grammatical gender should not be equated with biological sex. While terms for males are generally masculine and terms for women are generally feminine, the gender of most nouns has nothing to do with biological sex. (See MASCULINE; FEMININE; NEUTER.)

3. *Number.* Greek nouns are either singular, referring to one person or thing, or plural, referring to more than one person or things (see NUMBER; SINGULAR; PLURAL). Normally in Greek, the number of the verb will agree with the number of the subject.

An Exegetical Insight

Greek, unlike English, is a highly inflected language. What this means is that the function of nouns in Greek is shown through *the change in their case form* rather than through word order. In English, the sentence, "God loves the world" would be completely changed by reversing its word order: "The world loves God." In Greek, however, *case* rather than word order determines function. Note these examples:

ὁ θεὸς ἀγαπᾷ τὸν κόσμον.
τὸν κόσμον ἀγαπᾷ ὁ θεός.

Both sentences mean the same thing ("God loves the world"). It is not word order, but inflection, that determines the subject and the direct object.

Inflection can be a useful tool for Greek authors, since they can use word order for rhetorical impact rather than to show the function of a word. Consider John 1:18: Θεὸν οὐδεὶς ἑώρακεν πώποτε ("No one has ever seen God"). Since the subject "no one" (οὐδεὶς) is indicated by the nominative case instead of by word order, the author can bring the direct object "God" to the front of the sentence for emphasis.

NUMBERS, CARDINAL

What It Looks Like

The Greek cardinal numbers one through twelve and select others (20, 50, 100, 500, 1000) are shown here. Greek does not have unique numeral characters, instead using a letter with a hash mark (Aʹ).[1] These numerals do not usually occur in the New Testament, except in titles of book names (1 Corinthians = ΠΡΟΣ ΚΟΡΙΝΘΙΟΥΣ Αʹ).

The cardinal number εἷς ("one") declines in a 3-1-3 pattern. This means the masculine and neuter follow the third declension, while the feminine follows the first declension (for declension, see NOUN). The feminine form (μία) comes from a different root word.

Cardinal Numbers		Numerals	
εἷς	one	Αʹ	1
δύο	two	Βʹ	2
τρεῖς	three	Γʹ	3
τέσσαρες	four	Δʹ	4
πέντε	five	Εʹ	5
ἕξ	six	Ϛʹ	6
ἑπτά	seven	Ζʹ	7
ὀκτώ	eight	Η	8
ἐννέα	nine	Θʹ	9
δέκα	ten	Ιʹ	10
ἕνδεκα	eleven	ΙΑʹ	11
δώδεκα	twelve	ΙΒʹ	12
εἴκοσι	twenty	Κʹ	20
πεντήκοντα	fifty	Νʹ	50
ἑκατόν	hundred	Ρʹ	100
πεντακόσιοι	five hundred	Φʹ	500
χίλιοι	thousand	‚Α	1000

εἷς (3-1-3 adjective)

	Masc.	Fem.	Neut.
Nom. Sg.	εἷς	μία	ἕν
Gen. Sg.	ἑνός	μιᾶς	ἑνός
Dat. Sg.	ἑνί	μιᾷ	ἑνί
Acc. Sg.	ἕνα	μίαν	ἕν

The numbers two, three, and four are either indeclinable or follow the third declension. Numbers five through ten are indeclinable. Of course, all numbers except "one" are plural.

---

1. Rodney J. Decker, *Reading Koine Greek: An Introduction and Integrated Workbook* (Grand Rapids: Baker Academic, 2014), 623–24.

What It Does

Cardinal numbers express an amount, like one, two, three, etc. This may be contrasted with ordinal numbers (see NUMBERS, ORDINAL), which express degree or position in a series (first, second, third, etc.).

An Exegetical Insight

Numbers can carry symbolic as well as literal meaning. The number twelve (12), for example, often points symbolically to the twelve tribes of Israel. When Jesus chose twelve disciples, he was almost certainly in some sense claiming to reconstitute or restore the nation Israel.

The book of Revelation is full of symbolic numbers. The number seven, for example, occurs repeatedly. There are seven letters to churches (1:4), seven spirits before God's throne (1:4; 3:1; 4:5), seven golden lampstands (1:12, 20; 2:1), seven stars (1:16, 20; 2:1), seven horns and eyes on the Lamb (5:6), seven seals (5:1), seven trumpets (8:2, 6), seven bowls (15:7; 16:1; 17:1; 21:9), etc. The number seven often indicates completeness in Scripture.

The number six also plays an important role with reference to the number of the beast—666 (Rev 13:18). The number is called "the number of a man" and may indicate humanity falling short of God's perfection. Others propose that 666 is *gematria*, a practice of the rabbis that used numbers to represent names. When the name "Caesar Nero(n)" is transliterated into Hebrew (קסר נרון), its numeric value comes out to 666 (Caesar is ק = 100, ס = 60, ר = 200; Neron is נ = 50, ר = 200, ו = 6, ן = 50). The beast could in this way be associated with Nero, the evil emperor who instigated the first systematic persecution against the church.[2]

---

2. For details, see Grant R. Osborne, *Revelation*, BECNT (Grand Rapids: Baker, 2002), 518–21. Students should be cautious, since *gematria* is easily manipulated and notoriously unreliable. For example, arriving at "Caesar Nero" requires calculating a *Hebrew* transliteration of a *Greek* form of a *Latin* name, and that with a known but unusual spelling of "Caesar" (קסר instead of קיסר)!

NUMBERS, ORDINAL

What It Looks Like

The first ten ordinal numbers are shown below. Ordinals decline in a 2-1-2 pattern, meaning the masculine and neuter are in the second declension and the feminine is in the first declension (for declension, see NOUN).

Ordinal Numbers

πρῶτος, -η, -ον	first, 1ˢᵗ
δεύτερος, -α, -ον	second, 2ⁿᵈ
τρίτος, -η, -ον	third, 3ʳᵈ
τέταρτος, -η, -ον	fourth, 4ᵗʰ
πέμπτος, -η, -ον	fifth, 5ᵗʰ
ἕκτος, -η, -ον	sixth, 6ᵗʰ
ἕβδομος, -η, -ον	seventh, 7ᵗʰ
ὄγδοος, -η, -ον	eighth, 8ᵗʰ
ἔνατος, -η, -ον	ninth, 9ᵗʰ
δέκατος, -η, -ον	tenth, 10ᵗʰ

πρῶτος (2-1-2 adjective)

Case/ Num.	masc. 2	fem. 1	neut. 2
Nom. Sg.	πρῶτος	πρώτη	πρῶτον
Gen. Sg.	πρώτου	πρώτης	πρώτου
Dat. Sg.	πρώτῳ	πρώτῃ	πρώτῳ
Acc. Sg.	πρῶτον	πρώτην	πρῶτον
Nom. Pl.	πρῶτοι	πρῶται	πρῶτα
Gen. Pl.	πρώτων	πρώτων	πρώτων
Dat. Pl.	πρώτοις	πρώταις	πρώτοις
Acc. Pl.	πρώτους	πρώτας	πρῶτα

What It Does

Ordinal numbers express degree or position in a series (first, second, third, etc.). This may be contrasted with cardinal numbers (see NUMBERS, CARDINAL), which express an amount, like one, two, three, etc.

ὃς ἂν θέλῃ ἐν ὑμῖν εἶναι **πρῶτος** ἔσται πάντων δοῦλος·
"Whoever wishes to be **first** among you will be slave of all." (Mark 10:44)

ὥρα ἦν ὡς **ἕκτη**.
"It was about the **sixth** hour." (John 4:6)

The ordinal πρῶτος often functions as an adverb, meaning *first, in the first place, before, earlier, to begin with.*

ζητεῖτε δὲ **πρῶτον** τὴν βασιλείαν τοῦ θεοῦ καὶ τὴν δικαιοσύνην αὐτοῦ.
"Seek **first** the kingdom of God and his righteousness." (Matt 6:33)

In certain constructions the cardinal number "one" functions like an ordinal, meaning "first."[1]

καὶ λίαν πρωῒ **τῇ μιᾷ** τῶν σαββάτων.
"Very early **on the first day** of the week." (Mark 16:2)

An Exegetical Insight

The first twelve ordinal numbers appear together in Revelation 21:19–20, which names twelve precious stones decorating the walls of the New Jerusalem. The specific identity of some of these stones is debated:

οἱ θεμέλιοι τοῦ τείχους τῆς πόλεως παντὶ λίθῳ τιμίῳ κεκοσμημένοι· ὁ θεμέλιος **ὁ πρῶτος** ἴασπις,	The foundations of the city walls were adorned with every kind of precious stone. **The first** foundation was jasper,
ὁ δεύτερος σάπφιρος,	**the second** sapphire,
ὁ τρίτος χαλκηδών,	**the third** agate,
ὁ τέταρτος σμάραγδος,	**the fourth** emerald,
ὁ πέμπτος σαρδόνυξ,	**the fifth** onyx,
ὁ ἕκτος σάρδιον,	**the sixth** ruby [or, carnelian],
ὁ ἕβδομος χρυσόλιθος,	**the seventh** chrysolite,
ὁ ὄγδοος βήρυλλος,	**the eighth** beryl,
ὁ ἔνατος τοπάζιον,	**the ninth** topaz,
ὁ δέκατος χρυσόπρασος,	**the tenth** turquoise [or chrysoprase],
ὁ ἑνδέκατος ὑάκινθος,	**the eleventh** jacinth,
ὁ δωδέκατος ἀμέθυστος.	**the twelfth** amethyst.

---

1. BDAG, 293.

OPTATIVE

What It Looks Like

The optative mood is by far the rarest mood in the New Testament, occurring only 68 times, with almost one quarter of these appearing in the expression μὴ γένοιτο, "May it not be!" or "Absolutely not!" It occurs only in the present and the aorist in the New Testament. There is no epsilon augment (ε-) on the aorist optative, since the augment appears only in the indicative mood.

Main Forms of the Optative Mood (verbs: λύω; βάλλω; γράφω)

Present Active (λύω)		First Aorist Active (λύω)		Second Aor. Act. (βάλλω)	
Per. Sg.	Pl.	Per. Sg.	Pl.	Per. Sg.	Pl.
1ˢᵗ λύ οιμι	λύ οιμεν	1ˢᵗ λύ σαιμι	λύ σαιμεν	1ˢᵗ βάλοιμι	βάλοιμεν
2ⁿᵈ λύ οις	λύ οιτε	2ⁿᵈ λύ σαις	λύ σαιτε	2ⁿᵈ βάλοις	βάλοιτε
3ʳᵈ λύ οι	λύ οιεν	3ʳᵈ λύ σαι	λύ σαιεν	3ʳᵈ βάλοι	βάλοιεν
Present Middle/Passive		**First Aorist Middle**		**Second Aorist Middle**	
Per. Sg.	Pl.	Per. Sg.	Pl.	Per. Sg.	Pl.
1ˢᵗ λυ οίμην	λυ οίμεθα	1ˢᵗ λυ σαίμην	λυ σαίμεθα	1ˢᵗ βαλοίμην	βαλοίμεθα
2ⁿᵈ λύ οιο	λύ οισθε	2ⁿᵈ λύ σαιο	λύ σαισθε	2ⁿᵈ βάλοιο	βάλοισθε
3ʳᵈ λύ οιτο	λύ οιντο	3ʳᵈ λύ σαιτο	λύ σαιντο	3ʳᵈ βάλοιτο	βάλοιντο
		First Aorist Passive		**Second Aor. Pass. (γράφω)**	
		Per. Sg.	Pl.	Per. Sg.	Pl.
		1ˢᵗ λυ θείην	λυ θείμεν	1ˢᵗ γραφείην	γραφείημεν
		2ⁿᵈ λυ θείης	λυ θεῖτε	2ⁿᵈ γραφείης	γραφείητε
		3ʳᵈ λυ θείη	λύ θείησαν	3ʳᵈ γραφείη	γραφείησαν

What It Does

A mood is a feature of verbs that indicates the relationship between the verbal sense and reality. The optative mood is the mood of "wish" ("**May you perform** well!"). Contrast this with the INDICATIVE mood, the mood of reality ("I danced"), the SUBJUNCTIVE mood, the mood of potentiality ("I might dance"), and the IMPERATIVE mood, the mood of command ("Dance!"). The optative is sometimes viewed as a weakened form of the subjunctive. In Koine Greek, it was being gradually replaced by the subjunctive mood and was used only in stereotyped expressions. The following are the main functions of the optative in the New Testament:

1. *Voluntative Optative.* Used to express a wish or prayer.

> μὴ ἡ ἀπιστία αὐτῶν τὴν πίστιν τοῦ θεοῦ καταργήσει; **μὴ γένοιτο·**
> "Their unfaithfulness will not nullify the faithfulness of God, will it?
> **May it never be!**" (Rom 3:3–4)

2. *Deliberative (or Oblique) Optative.* Used to express an indirect question.

> Προσδοκῶντος δὲ τοῦ λαοῦ . . . μήποτε αὐτὸς **εἴη** ὁ χριστός.
> "The people were wondering . . . whether **he might be** the Christ."
> (Luke 3:15)

3. *In Conditional Sentences.* The optative occasionally occurs in fourth class conditions (see CONJUNCTION, CONDITIONAL), either in the protasis (a *conditional optative*) or in the apodosis (a *potential optative*).

- *Conditional optative:*

> εἰ καὶ **πάσχοιτε** διὰ δικαιοσύνην, μακάριοι.
> "Even if **you suffer** for what is right, you are blessed." (1 Pet 3:14)

- *Potential optative:*

> πῶς γὰρ ἂν **δυναίμην** ἐὰν μή τις ὁδηγήσει με;
> "How **can I** [understand] if someone does not guide me?" (Acts 8:31)

An Exegetical Insight

The stereotypical expression μὴ γένοιτο appears fifteen times in the New Testament, fourteen of which appear in Paul. It usually expresses strong revulsion or opposition to an idea. A "literal" rendering might be something like, "May it not be" or "May it not happen." It is interesting to see how various English versions handle it (Romans 3:4): "God forbid" (KJV); "Not at all!" (NIV); "May it never be!" (NASB); "By no means!" (ESV); "Absolutely not!" (HCSB); "Of course not!" (NLT); "Not on your life!" (MSG).

PARTICIPLE

What It Looks Like

The New Testament contains over 6,600 participles. The Greek participle is formed from the verbal stem, a participle morpheme, and a case ending. The present participle is provided below as an example. (For the participle morphemes of the other tenses, consult a grammar.)

Present Active Participle
(genitive singular masculine/neuter; verb: λύω)

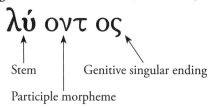

λύ οντ ος

Stem | Genitive singular ending

Participle morpheme

Case	Present Active			Case	Present Middle/Passive		
Sg.	M (3)	F (1)	N (3)	Sg.	M (2)	F (1)	N (2)
Nom.	λύων	λύουσα	λῦον	Nom.	λυόμενος	λυομένη	λυόμενον
Gen.	λύοντος	λυούσης	λύοντος	Gen.	λυομένου	λυομένης	λυομένου
Dat.	λύοντι	λυούσῃ	λύοντι	Dat.	λυομένῳ	λυομένη	λυομένῳ
Acc.	λύοντα	λύουσαν	λῦον	Acc.	λυόμενον	λυομένην	λυόμενον
Pl.				Pl.			
Nom.	λύοντες	λύουσαι	λύοντα	Nom.	λυόμενοι	λυόμεναι	λυόμενα
Gen.	λυόντων	λυουσῶν	λυόντων	Gen.	λυομένων	λυομένων	λυομένων
Dat.	λύουσι(ν)	λυούσαις	λύουσι(ν)	Dat.	λυομένοις	λυομέναις	λυομένοις
Acc.	λύοντας	λυούσας	λύοντα	Acc	λυομένους	λυομένας	λυόμενα

What It Does

A participle is a verbal adjective. In English the present participle is formed by adding "-ing" to the verbal stem: "talking," "going," "eating," "running." Like a verb, the participle has *tense* and *voice*. Like a noun, it has *case*, *number*, and *gender*.

Participles can function *attributively* (modifying a substantive), *substantivally* (functioning as a noun), or *adverbially* (modifying a verb). When a participle has the article, it is either attributive or substantival. The following are some of the main functions of the participle:

1. *Attributive (Modifying a Substantive).*

   ὁ ἀμνὸς τοῦ θεοῦ **ὁ αἴρων** τὴν ἁμαρτίαν τοῦ κόσμου
   "the lamb of God **who takes away** the sin of the world" (John 1:29)

2. *Substantival (Functioning as a Noun).*

   ὁ πέμψας με βαπτίζειν . . . εἶπεν
   "**The one who sent** me to baptize . . . said . . ." (John 1:33)

3. *Adverbial (Modifying a Verb).*

   • Temporal

   Ταῦτα εἶπεν ἐν συναγωγῇ **διδάσκων**.
   "He said these things, **while teaching** in the synagogue." (John 6:59)

   • Causal

   πλανᾶσθε **μὴ εἰδότες** τὰς γραφὰς.
   "You are in error **because you do not know** the Scriptures." (Matt 22:29)

   • Conditional

   θερίσομεν **μὴ ἐκλυόμενοι**.
   "We will reap **if we do not give up**." (Gal 6:9)

   • Concessive

   γράφω . . . **ἐλπίζων** ἐλθεῖν πρὸς σὲ ἐν τάχει.
   "I am writing . . . **although I hope** to come to you soon." (1 Tim 3:14)

   • Modal (manner)

   τρέμουσα ἦλθεν.
   "She came **trembling**." (Luke 8:47)

An Exegetical Insight

While adverbial participles are *grammatically* subordinate to the main verb, at times they express actions that are coordinate (parallel) rather than subordinate to the action of the main verb. These are called *attendant circumstances* or *circumstantial* participles, and are usually translated as finite verbs.

ἄρχων εἷς **ἐλθὼν** προσεκύνει αὐτῷ.
"A ruler **came and** bowed down to him." (Matt 9:18)

καθίσας ταχέως γράψον πεντήκοντα.
"**Sit down** quickly **and** write fifty." (Luke 16:6)

PARTICLE

What It Looks Like

There is no special form or inflection for particles. They are small, uninflected function words. The following are some of the most common particles in the New Testament and their function. Frequency numbers indicate total occurrences of the word in the New Testament. In some of these occurrences they may be functioning differently (e.g., as ADVERBs or CONJUNCTIONs).

Particle	Type	Meaning	Frequency
ἄν	contingent	ever, until (often untranslated)	166
γέ	emphatic	even, indeed	26
δέ	alternating	on the other hand	2791
ἐάν	contingent	ever (often untranslated)	334
ἤ	comparative	or, than, either . . . or	343
μέν	alternating	indeed, on the one hand	179
μή	negative	not, lest	1042
ναί	affirmation	yes	33
οὐ	negative	not, no	1648
πότε	interrogative	when?	48
ποῦ	interrogative	where?	52
πῶς	interrogative	how? in what way?	118
ὡς	comparative	as, like, while	504
ὡσεί	comparative	as, like, about	21
ὥσπερ	comparative	as, just as, like	36

What It Does

Particles are small words that serve a functional or relational role. Sometimes the term *particle* is used inclusively of all words that are not nouns, verbs, or adjectives, *including* PREPOSITIONs, CONJUNCTIONs, ARTICLEs, INTERJECTIONs, and other small words. Other times the term is defined exclusively of functional words that are *not* prepositions, conjunctions, adverbs, articles, or interjections. Particles and adverbs are sometimes difficult to distinguish, and they overlap considerably.

An Exegetical Insight

Because particles are primarily function words, they often have very little meaning content, making them a challenge to translate. The particle ἄν, for example, is a word that makes something contingent, indefinite, or potential that would normally be definite or real. When combined with the relative pronoun ὅς ("who"), for example, ἄν indicates a generic or unspecified person ("whoever" or "anyone"):

ὃς **ἂν** ἓν τῶν τοιούτων παιδίων δέξηται ἐπὶ τῷ ὀνόματί μου, ἐμὲ δέχεται.
"**Whoever** welcomes one of these children in my name welcomes me." (Mark 9:37)

The word doesn't mean "ever," but the translation "whoever" communicates the indefinite quality introduced by ἄν.

The particle often appears in conditional sentences, since these by nature indicate potentiality rather than reality (see CONJUNCTION, CONDITIONAL). In Luke 10, for example, Jesus says that if the miracles performed in Chorazin and Bethsaida had been done in Tyre and Sidon, then:

πάλαι **ἂν** ἐν σάκκῳ καὶ σποδῷ καθήμενοι μετενόησαν.
"they **would have** long ago repented, sitting in sackcloth and ashes." (Luke 10:13)

Without the word ἄν, this clause would mean, "they long ago repented . . ." What would otherwise be actual is made potential by ἄν. We could not say that ἄν *means* "would have," but its contingent sense is communicated with this expression in English (a conditional perfect tense).

PASSIVE

What It Looks Like

Since the passive voice is a feature of all the verbal moods (INDICATIVE, SUBJUNCTIVE, IMPERATIVE, OPTATIVE) and verbals (PARTICIPLE, INFINITIVE), there are a great many forms the passive voice can take. The following are the passive forms in the INDICATIVE mood. For passive forms in other moods and verbals, see their particular entries.

Passive Indicative in Various Tenses (λύω; λείπω)

Present Middle/Passive		Future Passive		Imperfect Middle/Passive	
Per. Sg.	Pl.	Per. Sg.	Pl.	Per. Sg.	Pl.
1st λύ ο μαι	λυ ό μεθα	1st λυ θή σ ο μαι	λυ θη σ ό μεθα	1st ἐ λυ ό μην	ἐ λυ ό μεθα
2nd λύ ῃ	λύ ε σθε	2nd λυ θή σ ῃ	λυ θή σ ε σθε	2nd ἐ λύ ου	ἐ λύ ε σθε
3rd λύ ε ται	λύ ο νται	3rd λυ θή σε ται	λυ θή σ ο νται	3rd ἐ λύ ε το	ἐ λύ ο ντο
Perfect Middle/Passive		**Pluperfect Middle/Passive**		**1st Aorist Passive**	
Per. Sg.	Pl.	Per. Sg.	Pl.	Per. Sg.	Pl.
1st λέ λυ μαι	λε λύ μεθα	1st ἐ λε λύ μην	ἐ λε λύ μεθα	1st ἐ λύ θη ν	ἐ λύ θη μεν
2nd λέ λυ σαι	λέ λυ σθε	2nd ἐ λέ λυ σο	ἐ λέ λυ σθε	2nd ἐ λύ θη ς	ἐ λύ θη τε
3rd λέ λυ ται	λέ λυ νται	3rd ἐ λέ λυ το	ἐ λέ λυ ντο	3rd ἐ λύ θη	ἐ λύ θη σαν
				2nd Aorist Passive	
				Per. Sg.	Pl.
				1st ἔ λιπ η ν	ἐ λίπ η μεν
				2nd ἔ λιπ η ς	ἐ λίπ η τε
				3rd ἔ λιπ η	ἐ λίπ η σαν

What It Does

The passive voice is one of three Greek voices: ACTIVE, MIDDLE, and PASSIVE. Voice indicates the relationship of the subject of a sentence to its verb, whether the subject is *acting* or *being acted upon*. In the active the subject is doing the action; in the passive, it is receiving the action. The agent of the action may or may not be stated.

1. *Simple Passive*. The subject receives the action of the verb.

> ἐβαπτίζοντο ὑπ᾽ αὐτοῦ ἐν τῷ Ἰορδάνῃ ποταμῷ.
> "**They were baptized** by him in the Jordan River." (Mark 1:5)

> ἐν ᾧ γὰρ πέπονθεν αὐτὸς **πειρασθείς**, δύναται τοῖς **πειραζομένοις** βοηθῆσαι.

"Because he himself suffered **when he was tempted**, he is able to help those **who are being tempted**." (Heb 2:18)

2. *Causative or Permissive Passive.* The subject permits, consents to, or causes the action of the verb.

Ταπεινώθητε οὖν ὑπὸ τὴν κραταιὰν χεῖρα τοῦ θεοῦ.
"**Allow yourself to be humbled**, therefore, under God's mighty hand." (1 Pet 5:6)

3. *Deponent Passive.* Most deponents in the New Testament are middles. But a few verbs are passive deponent, meaning passive in form but active in meaning (See MIDDLE voice).

ὁ δὲ οὐκ **ἀπεκρίθη** αὐτῇ λόγον.
"But he did not **answer** her a word." (Matt 15:23)

An Exegetical Insight

One of the most interesting uses of the passive in the New Testament is the "divine passive," where the unexpressed agent of a passive verb is God. In the Beatitudes in Matthew, μακάριοι οἱ πενθοῦντες, ὅτι αὐτοὶ παρακληθήσονται ("Blessed are those who mourn, for they will be comforted"; Matt 5:4) means "*for God will comfort them.*" Similarly, χορτασθήσονται ("they will be filled"; Matt 5:6) means "*God will fill them.*" These kinds of passives are common throughout the New Testament. The phrase δικαιούμενοι δωρεὰν τῇ αὐτοῦ χάριτι ("Being justified freely by his grace"; Rom 3:24) means, "*God* justifies freely by his grace."

In other cases, it is difficult to determine whether a divine passive is intended. Jesus repeatedly predicts that, "The Son of Man is going to be delivered [παραδίδοσθαι] into human hands" (Matt 17:22). While Jesus was betrayed by Judas and turned over to the Roman by the Jewish leaders, ultimately it was God himself who "delivered" Jesus to be crucified. Romans 4:25 makes this clear when we learn that Jesus "was delivered over [παρεδόθη] for our sins and was raised to life for our justification." This is clearly a divine passive. Although wicked people put Jesus to death, all along this was God's purpose and plan to accomplish his salvation (see Acts 2:23; 3:18; 4:28).

PERFECT

What It Looks Like

The perfect tense in the indicative is formed with a prefix reduplicating the initial consonant followed by an epsilon (e.g., λε- for λύω), and a suffix tense formative kappa (κ) with the secondary personal endings (the endings on aorist, imperfect, and perfect verbs). The perfect does not use connecting vowels. Vowels at the beginning of verbs usually lengthen rather than reduplicating.

Perfect Active Indicative (1st person singular; verb: λύω)

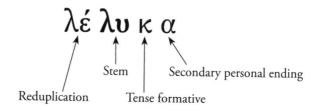

Reduplication · Stem · Tense formative · Secondary personal ending

Perfect Indicative Paradigm (verb: λύω)

Active			Middle/Passive		
Per.	Sg.	Pl.	Per.	Sg.	Pl.
1st	λέ λυ κ α	λε λύ κ α μεν	1st	λέ λυ μαι	λε λύ μεθα
2nd	λέ λυ κ ας	λε λύ κ α τε	2nd	λέ λυ σαι	λέ λυ σθε
3rd	λέ λυ κ ε(ν)	λέ λυ κ α ν (λελύκασι[ν])	3rd	λέ λυ ται	λέ λυ νται

What It Does

Tense in Greek can indicate the *time* of an action as well as *aspect*, the kind of action (see VERB). Aspect is always primary and time only becomes a factor in the INDICATIVE mood. The aspect of the perfect is *stative*, meaning it describes a state of affairs or condition that exists with no reference to change or progress. In the indicative mood the perfect tense generally indicates *completed action with continuing results*: "he has run." This contrasts with the aspect of other Greek past tenses in the indicative mood: the IMPERFECT tense indicates continuous past action ("he was running") while the AORIST tense indicates undefined or summary past action ("he ran").

Some common functions of the perfect in the New Testament are:

1. *Intensive perfect*, which emphasizes the resulting state of a past action.

   γέγραπται· οὐκ ἐπ᾽ ἄρτῳ μόνῳ ζήσεται ὁ ἄνθρωπος.
   "**It is written**: 'People shall not live on bread alone.'" (Matt 4:4)

2. *Consummative perfect*, or *extensive perfect*, which emphasizes the completed nature of the action.

   πεπληρώκατε τὴν Ἰερουσαλὴμ τῆς διδαχῆς ὑμῶν.
   "**You have filled** Jerusalem with your teaching." (Acts 5:28)

3. Perfect with present force.

   οὐκ **οἶδα** ὑμᾶς.
   "I do not **know** you." (Matt 25:12)

The verb οἶδα, which almost always carries this force, occurs 318 times in the NT. See also PLUPERFECT.

An Exegetical Insight

As the Greek tense that stresses past action with continuing results, the perfect tense is commonly used when an author is citing authoritative Scripture. The perfect tense is used almost a hundred times in this sense in the New Testament. Consider a few of these passages:

γέγραπται· ὁ οἶκός μου οἶκος προσευχῆς κληθήσεται . . .
"Just as **it is written**, 'My house will be called a house of prayer' . . . ."
(Matt 21:13, citing Isa 56:7)

ὡς καὶ ἐν τῷ ψαλμῷ **γέγραπται** τῷ δευτέρῳ· υἱός μου εἶ σύ, ἐγὼ σήμερον γεγέννηκά σε.
"As **it is written** in the second Psalm, 'You are my Son, today I have begotten you.'"
(Acts 13:33, citing Ps 2:7)

καθὼς **γέγραπται** ὅτι οὐκ ἔστιν δίκαιος οὐδὲ εἷς.
"Just as **it is written**: 'There is no one righteous, not even one.'" (Rom 3:10, citing Ps 14:1)

διότι **γέγραπται**· ἅγιοι ἔσεσθε, ὅτι ἐγὼ ἅγιος.
"For **it is written**: 'Be holy, because I am holy.'" (1 Pet 1:16, citing Lev 11:44)

The perfect tense stresses that Scripture, though written in the past, has continuing validity and authority for the people of God.

PERSON (1ˢᵀ, 2ᴺᴰ, 3ᴿᴰ)

What It Looks Like

Person can be indicated in Greek both in verbal endings and with pronouns. For details regarding the form of the personal verbal endings, see the corresponding entries under individual tenses (PRESENT, FUTURE, IMPERFECT, AORIST, PERFECT, PLUPERFECT) and moods (INDICATIVE, SUBJUNCTIVE, OPTATIVE, IMPERATIVE). The following are the personal pronouns in the first, second, and third persons:

1ˢᵗ Person, 2ⁿᵈ Person

1ˢᵗ Person		
Case	**Singular**	**Plural**
Nom.	ἐγώ I	ἡμεῖς we
Gen.	μου, ἐμοῦ my	ἡμῶν our
Dat.	μοι, ἐμοί to me	ἡμῖν to us
Acc.	με, ἐμέ me	ἡμᾶς us

2ⁿᵈ Person		
Case	**Singular**	**Plural**
Nom.	σύ you	ὑμεῖς you
Gen.	σου, σοῦ your	ὑμῶν your
Dat.	σοι, σοί to you	ὑμῖν to you
Acc.	σε, σέ you	ὑμᾶς you

3ʳᵈ Person

Singular				Plural		
Case	**Masc.**	**Fem.**	**Neut.**	**Masc.**	**Fem.**	**Neut.**
Nom.	αὐτός he/it	αὐτή she/it	αὐτό it	αὐτοί they	αὐταί they	αὐτά they
Gen.	αὐτοῦ of him/it	αὐτῆς of her/it	αὐτοῦ of it	αὐτῶν of them	αὐτῶν of them	αὐτῶν of them
Dat.	αὐτῷ to him/it	αὐτῇ to her/it	αὐτῷ to it	αὐτοῖς to them	αὐταῖς to them	αὐτοῖς to them
Acc.	αὐτόν him/it	αὐτήν her/it	αὐτό it	αὐτούς them	αὐτάς them	αὐτά them

What It Does

Grammatical person is a feature of verbs and pronouns that identifies the participants in an event, whether these participants include *the speaker* (first person; *I, we*), *the person(s) being spoken to* (second person; *you*), or *a third party being spoken about* (third person; *he, she, it, they*). Verbs in Greek carry their own person, so no separate subject pronoun is necessary. *Example:* λέγω = "I say"; first person singular verb. When a subject pronoun does appear, it is generally either redundant or emphatic.

An Exegetical Insight

As noted above, "person" identifies the person or persons involved in an event. Yet identification of person can be more complicated than this. Consider the distinction between the inclusive and exclusive "we." Sometimes "we" includes the person or persons being spoken to, and sometimes it excludes them. For example, if I say to my kids, "We are going to the party," I could mean my wife and I are going to the party without them (exclusive "we"), or I could mean that the whole family is going to the party (inclusive "we").

Consider 1 Thessalonians 1:2, where Paul says, "We always thank God for all of you" (NIV). By "we" he means that he and his companions pray for the Thessalonians. This is an exclusive "we." On the other hand, when James writes, "We all stumble in many ways" (Jas 3:2 NIV), he is obviously including the readers. This is an inclusive "we."

Although neither Greek, Hebrew, nor English distinguish in form between the exclusive and inclusive "we," many languages around the world do make this distinction. This creates a challenge for translators, who in each case must decide whether the "we" was intended to be inclusive or exclusive. Debated are verses like Romans 3:28: "For we maintain that a person is justified by faith apart from the works of the law" (NIV). Is this a point Paul himself is making (exclusive); or is he saying that this is a perspective "we Christians" affirm (inclusive)? In some languages, the translator must render a decision one way or the other. All translation involves interpretation.

PLUPERFECT

What It Looks Like

The pluperfect is by far the rarest of tenses in the New Testament, occurring only 86 times. The tense in the indicative is formed with the prefix (sometimes) of an epsilon augment (ε-), followed by reduplication of the initial consonant (λε-). The suffix has the tense formative kappa (κ) (sometimes), and a personal ending.

Pluperfect Active Indicative (1st person singular; verb: λύω)

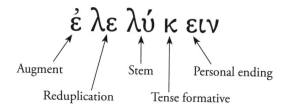

ἐ λε λύ κ ειν

Augment / Reduplication / Stem / Tense formative / Personal ending

Pluperfect Indicative Paradigm (verb: λύω)

Active		Middle/Passive		
Per. Sg.	Pl.	Per. Sg.	Pl.	
1ˢᵗ ἐ λε λύ κ ειν	ἐ λε λύ κ ει μεν	1ˢᵗ ἐ λε λύ μην	ἐ λε λύ μεθα	
2ⁿᵈ ἐ λε λύ κ εις	ἐ λε λύ κ ει τε	2ⁿᵈ ἐ λέ λυ σο	ἐ λέ λυ σθε	
3ʳᵈ ἐ λε λύ κ ει(ν)	ἐ λε λύ κ ει σαν	3ʳᵈ ἐ λέ λυ το	ἐ λέ λυ ντο	

What It Does

Tense in Greek can indicate the *time* of an action as well as *aspect*, the kind of action (see TENSE). Aspect is always primary and time only becomes a factor in the INDICATIVE mood. Like the PERFECT, the aspect of the pluperfect is *stative*, meaning it describes a state of affairs or condition that exists with no reference to change or progress. Yet the pluperfect is one step back from the perfect. For example, in the indicative the PERFECT tense often indicates completed action in the past ("he has run"), while the pluperfect indicates action *already completed* at some point in the past ("he had run").

There are two main functions of the pluperfect:

1. *Intensive Pluperfect.* This function emphasizes the continuing results of the past action. It is generally translated as a simple past or imperfect tense.

    οἱ δὲ ἄνδρες οἱ συνοδεύοντες αὐτῷ **εἰστήκεισαν** ἐνεοί.
    "The men traveling with him **stood** speechless." (Acts 9:7)

πάντες οἱ ἄγγελοι **εἰστήκεισαν** κύκλῳ τοῦ θρόνου.
"All the angels **were standing** around the throne." (Rev 7:11)

πτωχὸς δέ τις ὀνόματι Λάζαρος **ἐβέβλητο** πρὸς τὸν πυλῶνα αὐτοῦ.
"A certain poor man named Lazarus **was laid** at his gate." (Luke 16:20)

2. *Consummative Pluperfect.* This function emphasizes the completed nature of the action. It is usually translated with "had."

> **δεδώκει** δὲ ὁ παραδιδοὺς αὐτὸν σύσσημον αὐτοῖς.
> "His betrayer **had given** them a signal." (Mark 14:44)

> ἐδεῖτο δὲ αὐτοῦ ὁ ἀνὴρ ἀφ᾽ οὗ **ἐξεληλύθει** τὰ δαιμόνια εἶναι σὺν αὐτῷ.
> "The man from whom the demons **had gone out** begged him to go with him." (Luke 8:38)

An Exegetical Insight

Sometimes the meaning of a verb determines the choice of a particular tense. This is called *lexical intrusion.* The verb οἶδα, for example, is a PERFECT tense form which is commonly translated in English like a PRESENT ("I know"). This may be because the act of knowing has *a completed sense with continuing results*—a common function of the perfect tense. It is not surprising, then, that οἶδα is commonly used (33 times) in the pluperfect with the simple past sense of "knew":

ἐγὼ δὲ **ᾔδειν** ὅτι πάντοτέ μου ἀκούεις.
"**I knew** that you always hear me." (John 11:42)

εἰ **ᾔδει** ὁ οἰκοδεσπότης ποίᾳ ὥρᾳ ὁ κλέπτης ἔρχεται . . .
"If the owner of the house **knew** at what hour the thief was coming . . ."
(Luke 12:39)

Similarly, the verb ἵστημι ("I stand") often appears in the pluperfect (14 times). This is probably because the verb "stand" has the stative sense of a past action with continuing results. It is commonly translated as a simple past or an imperfect:

ἡ μήτηρ καὶ οἱ ἀδελφοὶ αὐτοῦ **εἰστήκεισαν** ἔξω ζητοῦντες αὐτῷ λαλῆσαι.
"His mother and brother **were standing** outside, trying to speak with him."
(Matt 12:46)

εἰστήκει ὁ Ἰησοῦς καὶ ἔκραξεν . . .
"Jesus **stood** and shouted . . ." (John 7:37)

Together, these two verbs, οἶδα (33x) and ἵστημι (14x), make up over half of the appearances of the pluperfect in the New Testament (86x).

PLURAL

What It Looks Like

Many parts of speech in Greek indicate number (singular and plural), including NOUNs, ADJECTIVEs, PRONOUNs, VERBs, and PARTICIPLEs. For details regarding the forms of the plural in each of these, see the corresponding entries in this resource.

What It Does

Greek has two number distinctions, singular (one) and plural (more than one). Some languages also have a dual form (two). Normally in Greek, the number of the verb will agree with the number of the subject:

ἠκολούθησαν [pl.] αὐτῷ οἱ μαθηταὶ [pl.].
"**The disciples followed** him." (Matt 8:23)

Yet there are some exceptions:

1. Neuter plural nouns in Greek sometimes take singular verbs.

   τὰ ἔργα [pl.] αὐτοῦ πονηρὰ ἦν [sg.].
   "His **works were** evil." (1 John 3:12)

2. Collective singular subjects occasionally take a plural verb.

   Καὶ ἦν ὁ λαὸς [sg.] προσδοκῶν τὸν Ζαχαρίαν καὶ ἐθαύμαζον [pl.] ἐν τῷ χρονίζειν ἐν τῷ ναῷ αὐτόν.
   "**The people** were waiting for Zechariah and **were wondering** why he was so long in the temple." (Luke 1:21)

   πᾶς ὁ ὄχλος [sg.] ἐζήτουν [pl.] ἅπτεσθαι αὐτοῦ.
   "**The** whole **crowd was seeking** to touch him." (Luke 6:19)

3. Compound subjects occasionally take singular verbs when one subject is highlighted.

   ἐκλήθη [sg.] δὲ καὶ ὁ Ἰησοῦς καὶ οἱ μαθηταὶ αὐτοῦ εἰς τὸν γάμον.
   "**Jesus (and his disciples) was invited** to the wedding." (John 2:2)

For more on number and agreement, see SINGULAR.

An Exegetical Insight

One significant difference between contemporary English and New Testament Greek is that English has lost its number distinctions in second person pronouns. In Old and Middle English, the second person singular pronouns were *thou* (subject), *thee* (object) and *thine* (possessive). The subjective form of the second person plural was *ye*. In contemporary English, however, we use *"you"* for all of these.

Because of this, some distinctions made in Greek are difficult to see in English. Consider John 1:50–51, where Jesus says to Nathaniel:

50 ὅτι εἶπόν **σοι** [sg.] ὅτι εἶδόν **σε** [sg.] ὑποκάτω τῆς συκῆς, **πιστεύεις** [sg.]; μεῖζω τούτων **ὄψῃ** [sg.]. 51 καὶ λέγει αὐτῷ· ἀμὴν ἀμὴν λέγω **ὑμῖν** [pl.], **ὄψεσθε** [pl.] τὸν οὐρανὸν ἀνεῳγότα καὶ τοὺς ἀγγέλους τοῦ θεοῦ ἀναβαίνοντας καὶ καταβαίνοντας ἐπὶ τὸν υἱὸν τοῦ ἀνθρώπου.

50 "**You believe** because I told **you** that I saw **you** under the fig tree. **You will see** greater things than that." 51 He then said to him, "Very truly I tell **you, you will see** 'heaven open, and the angels of God ascending and descending on' the Son of Man."

Whereas in English, all the second person words are translated "you," in Greek the pronouns and verbs in verse 50 are second person *singular*, while those in verse 51 are second person *plural*. So Jesus tells Nathanael that he saw him under the fig tree and that Nathanael would see greater things than this. But he then says that *all the disciples* will see heaven open and the angels of God ascending and descending on the Son of Man. This is an allusion to Jacob's dream in Genesis 28:12 and indicates that Jesus is the self-revelation of the Father, the ultimate connection between God and humanity and between heaven and earth.

PREPOSITION

What It Looks Like

The following are the twelve most common prepositions in the Greek New Testament and their most common meanings with various cases. Prepositions are uninflected with reference to case, number, gender, but sometimes change their form for phonetic reasons (pronunciation). The first column below shows the preposition when a word beginning with a consonant follows it. The second column is the form when a word follows beginning with a vowel or diphthong with a smooth breathing mark (ἀ). The third column is the form when a word follows beginning with a vowel or diphthong with a rough breathing mark (ἁ).

Twelve Most Common Prepositions in the New Testament

Preposition	Vowel w/ '	Vowel w/ '	Occurences	Translation
ἐν	ἐν	ἐν	2,752	*Dative*: in, at, by, on, to, with
εἰς	εἰς	εἰς	1,768	*Accusative*: into, in, toward, to, near, for
ἐκ	ἐξ	ἐξ	914	*Genitive*: out of, from, because of, of
ἐπί	ἐπ'	ἐφ'	890	*Genitive*: on, over, when *Dative*: on, in, at *Accusative*: on, for, to
πρός	πρός	πρός	700	*Accusative*: for, to, with, at, by, beside *Genitive*: for (1x) *Dative*: at (6x)
διά	δι'	δι'	667	*Genitive*: through, with, during, by, at *Accusative*: on account of, because of
ἀπό	ἀπ'	ἀφ'	646	*Genitive*: from, because of, away from, with, for
κατά	κατ'	καθ'	473	*Genitive*: down from, against *Accusative*: according to, along, to
μετά	μετ'	μεθ'	469	*Genitive*: with, among, against *Accusative*: after, behind
περί	περί	περί	333	*Genitive*: concerning, about *Accusative*: around, near
ὑπό	ὑπ'	ὑφ'	220	*Genitive*: by, at the hands of *Accusative*: under, below

παρά	παρ’	παρ’	194	*Genitive*: from *Dative*: beside, in the presence of *Accusative*: alongside, at, on, more than
ὑπέρ	ὑπέρ	ὑπέρ	150	*Genitive*: for, in behalf of, about *Accusative*: above, beyond, than
σύν	σύν	σύν	128	*Dative*: with, together with, besides
πρό	πρό	πρό	47	*Genitive*: before, in front of, at, above

What It Does

A preposition is a word that describes the relationship between other words in a sentence. This relationship is usually adverbial, though it can also be adjectival. In English, words like *in, at, to, with, by, of, for* are prepositions. Prepositions are part of a prepositional phrase, which includes the preposition plus a modifying noun, pronoun, or other substantive: "in the house"; "beside the table"; "after the lecture"; "around three o'clock." The modifying noun is known as the *object of the preposition*.

An Exegetical Insight

One of the most theologically significant prepositions in the New Testament is ἀντί, which occurs only twenty times. Scholars debate the meaning of ἀντί in Mark 10:45 (and its parallel in Matt 20:28):

κα γὰρ ὁ υἱὸς τοῦ ἀνθρώπου οὐκ ἦλθεν διακονηθῆναι ἀλλὰ διακονῆσαι καὶ δοῦναι τὴν ψυχὴν αὐτοῦ λύτρον **ἀντὶ** πολλῶν.

"For even the Son of Man did not come to be served, but to serve, and to give his life as a ransom **for/on behalf of/in place of** many." (Mark 10:45)

Some scholars claim that ἀντί here is equivalent to ὑπέρ, and means simply "on behalf of." In this case the passage teaches that Christ's death was in some sense for our benefit. Others argue that the meaning "in place of" or "in exchange for" is more likely, and that the passage teaches substitutionary atonement. Christ died in our place.

Both senses are possible (BDAG, 87), but "in place of" is the more common meaning of ἀντί and the one that best fits the context. In Matthew 2:22, Archelaus is said to be reigning "in place of" (ἀντί) his father Herod (not for his benefit—Herod is dead!), and in Matthew 5:38, Jesus cites the Old Testament law, "Eye for [ἀντί] eye, and tooth for [ἀντί] tooth" (cf. Exod 21:24). Furthermore, in collocational relationship with "ransom" (λύτρον), the word clearly has the sense of a payment that is *in exchange for or in place of* the person who is freed. Christ's death on the cross set us free by paying the penalty that we deserved.

PRESENT

What It Looks Like

Present tense verbs in the indicative mood are the easiest verbs to recognize, since the lexical form of a verb (the one you look up in a lexicon) is the present active indicative first person singular (λύω). The present tense is built with the first principal part verbal stem (see VERB), a connecting vowel (ε or ο), and the primary personal endings (the endings on present and future verbs). The indicative is shown below. For present tense forms in other moods and verbals, see SUBJUNCTIVE, IMPERATIVE, OPTATIVE, PARTICIPLE, INFINITIVE.

Present Active Indicative (1st person plural; verb: λύω)

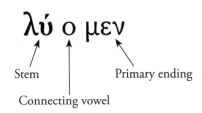

Present Indicative Paradigm (verb: λύω)

Active			Middle/Passive		
Per.	Sg.	Pl.	Per.	Sg.	Pl.
1ˢᵗ	λύ ω	λύ ο μεν	1ˢᵗ	λύ ο μαι	λυ ό μεθα
2ⁿᵈ	λύ ει ς	λύ ε τε	2ⁿᵈ	λύ ῃ	λύ ε σθε
3ʳᵈ	λύ ει	λύ ου σι(ν)	3ʳᵈ	λύ ε ται	λύ ο νται

What It Does

Tense in Greek can indicate the *time* of an action as well as *aspect,* the kind of action (see VERB). Time becomes a factor only in the INDICATIVE mood, where the present tense generally indicates *present time* (but see the *historical present* below). Even here, however, aspect is primary. The aspect of the present tense is *imperfective,* focusing on the internal progress or process of the action. (See also AORIST, IMPERFECT, and PERFECT.)

Some of the more common functions of the present tense include:

1. *Instantaneous Present.* This use of the present represents an action as completed at the moment of speaking.

> τέκνον, **ἀφίενταί** σου αἱ ἁμαρτίαι.
> "Son, your sins **are forgiven**." (Mark 2:5)

2. *Iterative Present.* Indicates the repeated nature of an action.

> τινὲς μὲν καὶ διὰ φθόνον καὶ ἔριν, τινὲς δὲ καὶ δι᾽ εὐδοκίαν τὸν Χριστὸν **κηρύσσουσιν**.
> "Some [repeatedly] **preach** Christ out of envy and rivalry, but others out of goodwill." (Phil 1:15)

3. *Gnomic Present.* Indicates a universal, timeless, or proverbial sense.

> ἱλαρὸν γὰρ δότην **ἀγαπᾷ** ὁ θεός.
> "For God **loves** a cheerful giver." (2 Cor 9:7)

4. *Conative Present.* Indicates something desired or intended.

> οἵτινες ἐν νόμῳ **δικαιοῦσθε**
> "those who are **attempting to be justified** by the Law" (Gal 5:4)

5. *Historical Present.* A present tense used in narrative to indicate a past action, often giving the story a vivid and lively style.

> Καὶ εὐθὺς τὸ πνεῦμα αὐτὸν **ἐκβάλλει** εἰς τὴν ἔρημον.
> "And immediately the Spirit **compels** him to go into the wilderness." (Mark 1:12)

An Exegetical Insight

All translation involves interpretation and *good* translation requires *good* interpretation. The conative function of the present tense illustrates this well. If the verb ἄγει in Romans 2:4 were translated as a simple present, it would read, "God's kindness **leads** you to repentance" (τὸ χρηστὸν τοῦ θεοῦ εἰς μετάνοιάν σε **ἄγει**). This, of course, is not always true. Though God is kind and good to all, many refuse to respond in repentance. This is clearly a conative present, indicating God's desire or the intended response to his kindness: "God's kindness *is intended to lead* you to repentance."

PRONOUN, DEMONSTRATIVE

What It Looks Like

The near demonstrative οὗτος is by far the most common demonstrative pronoun in the New Testament, occurring 1,387 times. The far demonstrative ἐκεῖνος occurs 265 times. (A few other demonstratives occur, including τοιοῦτος, τοσοῦτος, and ὅδε.) οὗτος and ἐκεῖνος decline regularly in the first and second declensions:

Near Demonstrative οὗτος ("this," "these")

Case	Singular			Plural		
	Masc.	**Fem.**	**Neut.**	**Masc.**	**Fem.**	**Neut.**
Nom.	οὗτος this	αὕτη this	τοῦτο this	οὗτοι these	αὗται these	ταῦτα these
Gen.	τούτου of this	ταύτης of this	τούτου of this	τούτων of these	τούτων of these	τούτων of these
Dat.	τούτῳ to this	ταύτῃ to this	τούτῳ to this	τούτοις to these	ταύταις to these	τούτοις to these
Acc.	τοῦτον this	ταύτην this	τοῦτο this	τούτους these	ταύτας these	ταῦτα these

Far Demonstrative ἐκεῖνος ("that," "those")

Case	Singular			Plural		
	Masc.	**Fem.**	**Neut.**	**Masc.**	**Fem.**	**Neut.**
Nom.	ἐκεῖνος that	ἐκείνη that	ἐκεῖνο that	ἐκεῖνοι those	ἐκεῖναι those	ἐκεῖνα those
Gen.	ἐκείνου of that	ἐκείνης of that	ἐκείνου of that	ἐκείνων of those	ἐκείνων of those	ἐκείνων of those
Dat.	ἐκείνῳ to that	ἐκείνῃ to that	ἐκείνῳ to that	ἐκείνοις to those	ἐκείναις to those	ἐκείνοις to those
Acc.	ἐκεῖνον that	ἐκείνην that	ἐκεῖνο that	ἐκείνους those	ἐκείνας those	ἐκεῖνα those

What It Does

Pronouns are words that replace nouns in a sentence. Demonstrative pronouns point something out or identify it. The *near demonstrative* is οὗτος ("this," "these"). The *far demonstrative* is ἐκεῖνος ("that"; "those"). Demonstrative pronouns can also function as adjectives, modifying nouns by specifying or pointing them out ("this book"; "that pencil"). Demonstrative adjectives take the predicate (or anarthrous) position when they are adjectives; i.e., they do not occur after the article.

- *Near Demonstrative as Pronoun*:

  οὗτός ἐστιν ὁ υἱός μου ὁ ἀγαπητός.
  "**This** is my beloved son." (Matt 3:17)

- *Near Demonstrative as Adjective*:

  Ταῦτα τὰ ῥήματα ἐλάλησεν . . . διδάσκων ἐν τῷ ἱερῷ.
  "He spoke **these words** . . . while teaching in the temple courts." (John 8:20)

- *Far Demonstrative as Pronoun*:

  ἐκεῖνοι μὲν οὖν ἵνα φθαρτὸν στέφανον λάβωσιν.
  "**Those** receive a perishable crown." (1 Cor 9:25)

- *Far Demonstrative as Adjective*:

  ἰάθη ὁ παῖς αὐτοῦ ἐν τῇ ὥρᾳ **ἐκείνῃ**.
  "His servant was healed in **that** hour." (Matt 8:13)

An Exegetical Insight

The demonstrative pronoun is close in meaning to the personal pronoun, since both point to things. The difference is that personal pronouns are *anaphoric*, pointing back to an antecedent previously mentioned or implied, while the demonstrative points to something present. Yet these functions overlap, and Greek sometimes uses the demonstrative where English uses personal pronouns. Consider these examples:

οὗτος ἔσται μέγας καὶ υἱὸς ὑψίστου κληθήσεται.
"**He** will be great and will be called the Son of the Most High." (Luke 1:32)

οὗτος ἦν ἐν ἀρχῇ πρὸς τὸν θεόν.
"**He** was with God in the beginning." (John 1:2)

οὐκ ἦν **ἐκεῖνος** τὸ φῶς.
"**He** was not the light." (John 1:8)

PRONOUN, INDEFINITE

What It Looks Like

The Greek indefinite pronoun τις occurs 525 times in the New Testament. It has the same form as the interrogative pronoun τίς except that the interrogative has its accent on the first syllable while the indefinite pronoun either has no accent or the accent is on the second syllable. The pronoun τις declines in the third declension (for the meaning of declension, see NOUN).

Indefinite Pronoun τις

Case	Singular		Plural	
	Masc. & Fem.	Neut.	Masc. & Fem.	Neut.
Nom.	τις	τι	τινές	τινά
Gen.	τινός	τινός	τινῶν	τινῶν
Dat.	τινί	τινί	τισί(ν)	τισί(ν)
Acc.	τινά	τι	τινάς	τινά

What It Does

The indefinite pronoun τις introduces a general, unknown, or unidentified antecedent. It can be translated "anyone," "someone," "a certain one," "a certain thing." It can also identify *a member of a class*, without being more specific, as in the clause, **τις** τῶν νομικῶν λέγει αὐτῷ ("**One** of the experts in the law said to him"; Luke 11:45). It can also function adjectivally, in which case it is often translated "a certain [person/thing]" or "certain [people/things]" (see examples below).

- *Examples as Pronoun*:

  Ἠρώτα δέ **τις** αὐτὸν τῶν Φαρισαίων ἵνα φάγῃ μετ' αὐτοῦ . . .
  "When **one** of the Pharisees invited Jesus to eat with him . . ." (Luke 7:36)

  εἰσίν **τινες** ὧδε τῶν ἑστηκότων οἵτινες οὐ μὴ γεύσωνται θανάτου ἕως ἂν ἴδωσιν τὴν βασιλείαν τοῦ θεοῦ ἐληλυθυῖαν ἐν δυνάμει.
  "There are **some** of those standing here who will certainly not taste death until they see the kingdom of God come in power." (Mark 9:1)

  καὶ ἐάν **τις** ὑμῖν εἴπῃ **τι**, ἐρεῖτε ὅτι ὁ κύριος αὐτῶν χρείαν ἔχει.
  "If **anyone** says **anything** to you, say that the Lord needs them." (Matt 21:3)

  ὁ δὲ Ἰησοῦς εἶπεν· ἥψατό μού **τις**.
  "But Jesus said, '**Someone** touched me.'" (Luke 8:46)

Καί **τινες** κατελθόντες ἀπὸ τῆς Ἰουδαίας ἐδίδασκον . . .
"**Certain people** who came down from Judea were teaching . . ."
(Acts 15:1)

- *Examples as Adjective*:

Καὶ ἐγένετο ἐν τῷ εἶναι αὐτὸν ἐν **τόπῳ τινὶ** προσευχόμενον . . .
"And it came to pass while he was praying in a **certain place** . . ."
(Luke 11:1)

παρεισέδυσαν γάρ **τινες ἄνθρωποι.**
"**For certain people** snuck in secretly." (Jude 4)

γυναῖκές τινες αἳ ἦσαν τεθεραπευμέναι ἀπὸ πνευμάτων πονηρῶν καὶ
ἀσθενειῶν . . .
"**certain women** who were healed from evil spirits and diseases . . ."
(Luke 8:2)

An Exegetical Insight

The indefinite relative pronoun is commonly used in proverbial and wisdom literature since its generic quality is well suited for the general nature of proverbs. James, for examples, uses τις fifteen times in his short letter. Anyone (τις) who lacks wisdom should ask God to give it to them (1:5). Anyone (τις) who considers themselves religious should bridle their tongue (1:26). If someone (τις) claims to have faith, they should demonstrate it with their works (2:14). If one (τις) among you says, "Be warmed and filled," but does nothing to help the other person, what good is it? (2:16). The letter closes with a series of such exhortations:

Is anyone [τις] among you in trouble? Let them pray. Is anyone [τις] happy? Let them sing songs of praise. Is anyone [τις] among you sick? Let them call the elders of the church to pray over them. . . . My brothers and sisters, if one [τις] of you should wander from the truth and someone [τις] should bring that person back, remember this: Whoever turns a sinner from the error of their way will save them from death and cover over a multitude of sins. (Jas 5:13–14a, 19–20)

PRONOUN, INTERROGATIVE

The most common interrogative pronoun in the New Testament is τίς, which occurs approximately 555 times. τίς has the same form as the indefinite pronoun τις except that it has its accent on the first syllable while the indefinite pronoun either has no accent or the accent is on the second syllable. τίς declines in the third declension (for declension, see NOUN).

Interrogative Pronoun τίς

Case	Singular		Plural	
	Masc. & Fem.	Neut.	Masc. & Fem.	Neut.
Nom.	τίς	τί	τίνες	τίνα
Gen.	τίνος	τίνος	τίνων	τίνων
Dat.	τίνι	τίνι	τίσι(ν)	τίσι(ν)
Acc.	τίνα	τί	τίνας	τίνα

Other interrogative pronouns include ποῖος ("what sort?"), πόσος ("how much?"), and ποταπός ("what sort of?").

What It Does

An *interrogative pronoun* introduces a question. English interrogative pronouns includes words like "What?" "Which?" "Who?" "Whose?" Unlike in English, where word order can indicate a question (compare: "You are going" with "Are you going?"), Greek does not use word order to indicate a question. Questions are signaled either by interrogative pronouns or by context. The Greek question mark looks the same as an English semicolon (;).

τίνα μισθὸν ἔχετε;
"**What** reward will you get?" (Matt 5:46)

τίς τούτων τῶν τριῶν πλησίον δοκεῖ σοι . . . ;
"**Which** of these three do you think was a neighbor . . . ?" (Luke 10:36)

τίς εἶ, κύριε;
"**Who** are you, Lord?" (Acts 9:5)

An Exegetical Insight

Interrogative pronouns can introduce not only real questions, but also rhetorical ones. While real questions request information (e.g., "How old are you?"), rhetorical questions are intended to make a point. For example, when Paul says in Romans 6:2, "We who have died to sin, how can we still live in it?" (οἵτινες ἀπεθάνομεν τῇ ἁμαρτίᾳ, πῶς ἔτι ζήσομεν ἐν αὐτῇ;), he is not asking for advice on how to keep living in sin. The rhetorical question means, "We must not keep living in sin!"

Some of the most powerful rhetorical questions in Paul's letters appear in the climax to his discussion of the certainty of salvation in Romans 8:31–39. Paul uses interrogative pronouns to ask four rhetorical questions:

1. εἰ ὁ θεὸς ὑπὲρ ἡμῶν, **τίς** καθ' ἡμῶν;
   "If God is for us, **who** can be against us?" (v. 31)

2. **τίς** ἐγκαλέσει κατὰ ἐκλεκτῶν θεοῦ;
   "**Who** will bring a charge against God's elect?" (v. 33)

3. **τίς** ὁ κατακρινῶν;
   "**Who** is the one who condemns [God's people]?" (v. 34)

4. **τίς** ἡμᾶς χωρίσει ἀπὸ τῆς ἀγάπης τοῦ Χριστοῦ;
   "**What** shall separate us from the love of Christ?" (v. 35)

The answer to all these questions is a resounding, "No one and nothing!" Paul concludes by answering the last question with a powerful poetic conclusion:

> For I am convinced that
>> neither death nor life
>> neither angels nor rulers
>> neither things present nor things coming
>> nor powers
>> neither height nor depth
>> nor any other created thing
> will be able to separate us from the love of God
>> that is in Christ Jesus our Lord." (vv. 38–39)

PRONOUN, PERSONAL

What It Looks Like

Personal pronouns are by far the most common pronouns in the New Testament. There are approximately 11,170 of them. The following are the first, second, and third person pronouns:

1st Person and 2nd Person Personal Pronouns

1st Person			2nd Person		
Case	Singular	Plural	Case	Singular	Plural
Nom.	ἐγώ, I	ἡμεῖς, we	Nom.	σύ, you	ὑμεῖς, you
Gen.	μου, ἐμοῦ, my	ἡμῶν, our	Gen.	σου, σοῦ, your	ὑμῶν, your
Dat.	μοι, ἐμοί, to me	ἡμῖν, to us	Dat.	σοι, σοί, to you	ὑμῖν, to you
Acc.	με, ἐμέ, me	ἡμᾶς, us	Acc.	σε, σέ, you	ὑμᾶς, you

3rd Person Personal Pronouns

Case	Singular			Plural		
	Masc.	Fem.	Neut.	Masc.	Fem.	Neut.
Nom.	αὐτός he/it	αὐτή she/it	αὐτό it	αὐτοί they	αὐταί they	αὐτά they
Gen.	αὐτοῦ of him/of it	αὐτῆς of her/of it	αὐτοῦ of it	αὐτῶν of them	αὐτῶν of them	αὐτῶν of them
Dat.	αὐτῷ to him/to it	αὐτῇ to her/to it	αὐτῷ to it	αὐτοῖς to them	αὐταῖς to them	αὐτοῖς to them
Acc.	αὐτόν him/it	αὐτήν her/it	αὐτό it	αὐτούς them	αὐτάς them	αὐτά them

What It Does

Pronouns replace nouns in a sentence. The noun a pronoun replaces is called its *antecedent*. A *personal pronoun* is a pronoun that represents a particular person or thing (I, you, he, she, it, they). It is the "default" pronoun in that it simply refers to the person or thing without additional qualifiers, such as DEMONSTRATIVE, RELATIVE or INTERROGATIVE pronouns.

Since Greek verbs are already marked for PERSON and NUMBER (e.g., γράφω = 1st person singular: "I write"), no personal pronoun is necessary in the subject. When the pronoun does occur in the nominative, it is normally there for emphasis:

οὐχ **ὑμεῖς** με ἐξελέξασθε, ἀλλ᾽ **ἐγὼ** ἐξελεξάμην ὑμᾶς.
"**You** did not choose me, but **I** chose you." (John 15:16)

The third person pronoun αὐτός can function in three different ways:

1. *Personal Pronoun.* αὐτός most commonly functions as a personal pronoun (he, she, it, they; him, her, them). As noted above, it most commonly occurs in the oblique cases (GENITIVE [2157x], DATIVE [1545x], ACCUSATIVE [1620x]), rather than in the NOMINATIVE (275x), since Greek verbs are marked already for their subject (person and number).

2. *Intensive Adjective.* αὐτός can be used to add emphasis to a noun. This usage is normally translated in English with an emphatic pronoun (himself, herself, itself).

> **αὐτὸς** γὰρ Δαυὶδ λέγει ἐν βίβλῳ ψαλμῶν . . .
> "For David **himself** says in the Book of Psalms . . ." (Luke 20:42)

When functioning as an intensive adjective, αὐτός is normally in the predicate or anarthrous position (the article does not precede it).

3. *Identical Adjective.* αὐτός can also function as an identical adjective, where it is usually translated "the same."

> ὁ γὰρ **αὐτὸς** κύριος πάντων.
> "For the **same** Lord is Lord of all." (Rom 10:12)

When functioning as an intensive adjective, αὐτός generally takes the attributive position (if the article is present, it immediately precedes αὐτός).

An Exegetical Insight

The emphasis made through the adjectival intensive use of αὐτός makes this construction particularly appropriate for profound statements of theological truth. Consider these examples:

- *Adoption through the Spirit of God* (Rom 8:16)

> **αὐτὸ τὸ πνεῦμα** συμμαρτυρεῖ τῷ πνεύματι ἡμῶν ὅτι ἐσμὲν τέκνα θεοῦ.
> "**The Spirit himself** testifies with our spirit that we are God's children."

- *God's Sanctifying Work through the Spirit* (1 Thess 5:23)

> **Αὐτὸς** δὲ ὁ **θεὸς** τῆς εἰρήνης ἁγιάσαι ὑμᾶς ὁλοτελεῖς.
> "May **God himself**, the God of peace, sanctify you through and through."

PRONOUN, RELATIVE

What It Looks Like

The Greek relative pronoun ὅς occurs over 1500 times in the New Testament. It is similar in form to first and second declension endings of nouns and adjectives (see NOUN). All the forms begin with a rough breathing mark and have an accent (compare the ARTICLE).

Forms of the Relative Pronoun ὅς

Case	Singular Masc.	Fem.	Neut.	Plural Masc.	Fem.	Neut.	Translation
Nom.	ὅς	ἥ	ὅ	οἵ	αἵ	ἅ	who/which/that
Gen.	οὗ	ἧς	οὗ	ὧν	ὧν	ὧν	of whom/which/whose
Dat.	ᾧ	ᾗ	ᾧ	οἷς	αἷς	οἷς	to whom/which/whose
Acc.	ὅν	ἥν	ὅ	οὕς	ἅς	ἅ	whom/which/that

What It Does

Relative pronouns in English are words like "who," "that," "which," and "what." Every relative pronoun is part of a relative clause, which includes the relative pronoun embedded in a clause (a clause has a subject and a predicate). Relative clauses function as a part of speech in the sentence, either adjectivally (modifying a noun) or substantivally (like a noun):

1. *Adjectival Use.* Consider the following English sentences. The relative clause is underlined and the relative pronoun is bold.
   - The student **who** took the exam brought me his paper.
   - The student **whom** I can trust brought me his paper
   - The student **to whom** I gave the book brought me his paper.

In all three sentences, the relative clause is functioning *adjectivally*, modifying "the student." In the first, the relative pronoun ("who") is the subject of the relative clause ("*who* took the exam"). In the second, the relative pronoun ("whom") is the object of the relative clause ("I can trust *whom*"). In the third, the relative pronoun is functioning like the indirect object of the relative clause ("I gave the book *to whom*").

2. *Substantival Use.* In addition to modifying a noun, the relative clause can function as a noun (substantivally). Consider these sentences:

- **Whoever tries hardest** wins the game.
- The thieves took **what they wanted**.

In the first, the relative clause is the subject of the sentence (telling who won the game). In the second, the relative clause is the direct object of the sentence (telling what the thieves took).

Greek relative clauses function in the same way, whether adjectivally or substantivally. The case of the relative pronoun normally will depend on its function *within the relative clause.* Here are two examples of relative clauses and their function:

- *Substantival Relative Clause* (functioning as the subject of the sentence)

  ὃς οὐκ ἔστιν καθ᾽ ὑμῶν, ὑπὲρ ὑμῶν ἐστιν.
  "**Whoever is not against you** is for you." (Mark 9:40)

- *Adjectival Relative Clause* (modifying "light")

  ῏Ην τὸ φῶς τὸ ἀληθινόν, ὃ φωτίζει πάντα ἄνθρωπον.
  "He was the true light, **which shines on every person.**" (John 1:9)

An Exegetical Insight

A good example of the adjectival function of the relative clause appears in Paul's profound description of the gospel in 1 Corinthians 15:1–2:

Γνωρίζω δὲ ὑμῖν, ἀδελφοί, τὸ εὐαγγέλιον ὃ εὐηγγελισάμην ὑμῖν, ὃ καὶ παρελάβετε, ἐν ᾧ καὶ ἑστήκατε, δι᾽ οὗ καὶ σῴζεσθε, τίνι λόγῳ εὐηγγελισάμην ὑμῖν εἰ κατέχετε.

"Now, brothers and sisters, I remind you of the gospel, **which I preached to you, which also you received, on which also you have taken your stand, through which you are saved,** if you hold fast to the message preached to you."

The gospel (τὸ εὐαγγέλιον) is described with four relative clauses, all functioning adjectivally. They describe the essential factors for the good news to fulfill its role in the world. It must be *announced by the preacher* ("which I preached to you"); it must be *accepted by the hearer* ("which also you received"); it must be *held firm through trials* ("on which also you have taken your stand") until it achieves its result—our salvation ("through which you are saved").

PRONOUNS, OTHER

Reciprocal Pronoun

A reciprocal pronoun indicates that two or more people are carrying out a particular action and that both receive the benefits or consequences of that action. Reciprocal pronouns in English include "one another" or "each other." The most common reciprocal pronoun in the New Testament is ἀλλήλων, which occurs 100 times.

Ἀγαπητοί, ἀγαπῶμεν **ἀλλήλους**.
"Loved ones, let us love **one another**." (1 John 4:7)

τῇ φιλαδελφίᾳ εἰς **ἀλλήλους** φιλόστοργοι, τῇ τιμῇ **ἀλλήλους** προηγούμενοι.
"Be devoted to **one another** in brotherly love. Lead the way in honor to **one another**." (Rom 12:10)

Reflexive Pronoun

A reflexive action is one in which the subject and the object refer to the same person or thing. In reflexive constructions the subject generally acts on itself. The most common reflexive pronoun in Greek is ἑαυτοῦ, which occurs 319 times in the New Testament.

ἄλλους ἔσωσεν, **ἑαυτὸν** οὐ δύναται σῶσαι.
"He saved others, but he is not able to save **himself**." (Matt 27:42)

ὥσπερ γὰρ ὁ πατὴρ ἔχει ζωὴν **ἐν ἑαυτῷ**, οὕτως καὶ τῷ υἱῷ ἔδωκεν ζωὴν ἔχειν **ἐν ἑαυτῷ**.
"For just as the Father has life **in himself**, so he has granted the Son also to have life **in himself**." (John 5:26)

Μηδεὶς **ἑαυτὸν** ἐξαπατάτω.
"Let no one deceive **himself**." (1 Cor 3:18)

Possessive Pronoun

In English, possessive pronouns include words such as mine, yours, his, hers, its, theirs. For example: "That book is mine." Greek does not have a distinct class of possessive pronouns, using instead the GENITIVE case forms of the PERSONAL PRONOUN.

An Exegetical Insight

Perhaps the most famous reciprocal pronouns in the New Testament are those connected to the verb ἀγαπάω ("I love") in the Johannine literature. Three times in the Gospel of John (13:34 [2x], 35), five times in 1 John (3:11, 23; 4:7, 11, 12), and once in 2 John (v. 5), true believers are identified as those who love *one another*. This, more than anything else, is the distinguishing mark of a true believer.

John 13:35 sums it up well:

> ἐν τούτῳ γνώσονται πάντες ὅτι ἐμοὶ μαθηταί ἐστε,
> ἐὰν ἀγάπην ἔχητε ἐν ἀλλήλοις.
> "By this everyone will know that you are my disciples,
> if you have love for one another."

SINGULAR

What It Looks Like

Many parts of speech in Greek indicate number (singular and plural), including NOUNs, ADJECTIVEs, PRONOUNs, VERBs, and PARTICIPLEs. For details regarding the forms of the singular in each of these, see the corresponding entries in this resource.

What It Does

Greek has two number distinctions, singular (one) and plural (more than one). Some languages also have a dual form (two). An important aspect of number is *agreement*:

1. A VERB will agree with its subject in number, whether singular or plural.

   ὁ Ἰησοῦς [sg.] **εἶπεν** [sg.] αὐτῷ
   "**Jesus said** to him" (Luke 4:8)

   ἠκολούθησαν [pl.] αὐτῷ οἱ **μαθηταὶ** [pl.].
   "**The disciples followed** him." (Matt 8:23)

2. An ADJECTIVE will agree with the noun it modifies in number, whether singular or plural.

   ὁ **δράκων** [sg.] ὁ **μέγας** [sg.]
   "**the great dragon**" (Rev 12:9)

   ὄχλοι [pl.] **πολλοὶ** [pl.]
   "**great crowds**" (Luke 5:15)

3. A PRONOUN will agree with its antecedent in number, whether singular or plural.

   ὑμῖν πρῶτον ἀναστήσας ὁ **θεὸς** [sg.] τὸν παῖδα **αὐτοῦ** [sg.] ἀπέστειλεν αὐτὸν εὐλογοῦντα ὑμᾶς.
   "When **God** raised up **his** servant, he sent him first to you to bless you." (Acts 3:26)

   οἱ **Φαρισαῖοι** [pl.] καὶ οἱ γραμματεῖς **αὐτῶν** [pl.]
   "**the Pharisees** and **their** scribes" (Luke 5:30)

For some exceptions to the rules of agreement, see PLURAL.

An Exegetical Insight

The identification of number gets interesting with reference to Paul's letters, which are often identified as coming from both Paul and his companions. For example, 1 Thessalonians begins, "Paul, Silvanus, and Timothy, to the church of the Thessalonians" (Παῦλος καὶ Σιλουανὸς καὶ Τιμόθεος τῇ ἐκκλησίᾳ Θεσσαλονικέων; 1 Thess 1:1). Is the letter from Paul, or from Paul and his companions? In the letter itself, Paul uses first person singular verbs only twice ("I"; 3:5; 5:27), but first person plural ("we") forty-seven times. Although Paul is the primary writer, he clearly intends the letter to be read as coming from both him and his companions. Contrast this with 1 Corinthians (written "from Paul . . . and Sosthenes"; 1 Cor 1:1), which has 192 first-person singular verbs and only 71 first-person plurals.

Further complicating the issue is Paul's frequent use of the editorial or epistolary "we," where an author uses the first person plural to refer to himself. In 2 Corinthians 10:13 Paul is defending himself when he says, ἡμεῖς δὲ οὐκ εἰς τὰ ἄμετρα καυχησόμεθα ("We will not boast beyond proper limits"). It is clear from the context Paul is referring to himself. In other contexts, however, it is difficult to determine whether Paul is speaking of himself or of himself and others. Paul writes in 2 Corinthians 10:2, "I beg you that when I come I may not have to be as bold as I expect to be toward some people who think that we live by the standards of this world." Does the "we" here refer to Paul's behavior, or the behavior of Paul and his companions? It is hard to say. Sometimes a plural may actually mean singular! (see also PLURAL, PERSON)

SUBJUNCTIVE

What It Looks Like

The subjunctive mood has the same basic form as the INDICATIVE except that the connecting vowel is lengthened.

Subjunctive Mood Paradigm (verbs: λύω; λείπω)

Present Active (λύω)			**Aorist Active** (λύω)			**Second Aorist** (λείπω)		
Per.	Sg.	Pl.	Per.	Sg.	Pl.	Per.	Sg.	Pl.
1st	λύ ω	λύ ωμεν	1st	λύ σω	λύ σωμεν	1st	λίπ ω	λίπ ωμεν
2nd	λύ ῃς	λύ ητε	2nd	λύ σῃς	λύ σητε	2nd	λίπ ῃς	λίπ ητε
3rd	λύ ῃ	λύ ωσι(ν)	3rd	λύ σῃ	λύ σωσι(ν)	3rd	λίπ ῃ	λίπ ωσι(ν)
Present Middle/Passive			**Aorist Middle**			**Second Aorist Middle**		
Per.	Sg.	Pl.	Per.	Sg.	Pl.	Per.	Sg.	Pl.
1st	λύ ωμαι	λυ ώμεθα	1st	λύ σωμαι	λυ σώμεθα	1st	λίπ ωμαι	λίπ ώμεθα
2nd	λύ ῃ	λύ ησθε	2nd	λύ σῃ	λύ σησθε	2nd	λίπ ῃ	λίπ ησθε
3rd	λύ ηται	λύ ωνται	3rd	λύ σηται	λύ σωνται	3rd	λίπ ηται	λίπ ωνται
			Aorist Passive			**Second Aorist Passive**		
			Per.	Sg.	Pl.	Per.	Sg.	Pl.
			1st	λυ θῶ	λυ θῶμεν	1st	λιπ ῶ	λιπ ῶμεν
			2nd	λυ θῇς	λυ θῆτε	2nd	λιπ ῆς	λιπ ῆτε
			3rd	λυ θῇ	λύ θῶσι(ν)	3rd	λιπ ῇ	λιπ ῶσι(ν)

What It Does

Mood indicates the relationship of a verb's action to reality. The subjunctive mood is the mood of potentiality and is often translated as "may" or "might" ("He might run.") Contrast this with the INDICATIVE mood, the mood of reality (*Example*: "He ran."). The following are some of the primary functions of the subjunctive.

1. *In Main (Independent) Clauses.*

   • *Hortatory Subjunctive.* Used to exhort or encourage others to a particular action.

     Σπουδάσωμεν . . . εἰσελθεῖν εἰς ἐκείνην τὴν κατάπαυσιν.
     "**Let us strive** . . . to enter that rest." (Heb 4:11)

   • *Deliberative Subjunctive.* Raises a question which is used to consider a course of action. The question can be real or rhetorical.

Μὴ οὖν μεριμνήσητε λέγοντες· τί **φάγωμεν**;
"So do not worry, saying, 'What **shall we eat?**'" (Matt 6:31)

- *Emphatic Negation Subjunctive.* οὐ μή + aorist subjunctive indicates strong negation.

  οὐ μὴ **φάγω** κρέα εἰς τὸν αἰῶνα.
  "**I will certainly** never **eat** meat again." (1 Cor 8:13)

2. *In Subordinate (Dependent) Clauses.*

- ἵνα *Clauses.* This is the most common use in the New Testament.

  τὸ λογικὸν ἄδολον γάλα ἐπιποθήσατε, ἵνα ἐν αὐτῷ **αὐξηθῆτε** εἰς σωτηρίαν.
  "Crave pure spiritual milk, so that by it **you may grow up** into salvation." (1 Pet 2:2)

- *Conditional Clauses.* Subjunctive used in third class conditions.

  ἐὰν **εἴπωμεν** ὅτι ἁμαρτίαν οὐκ ἔχομεν, ἑαυτοὺς πλανῶμεν.
  "**If we say** that we are without sin, we deceive ourselves." (1 John 1:8)

An Exegetical Insight

One of the most exegetically significant examples of a hortatory subjunctive occurs in a textual variant in Romans 5:1. While some manuscripts read εἰρήνην **ἔχομεν** πρὸς τὸν θεὸν διὰ τοῦ κυρίου ἡμῶν Ἰησοῦ Χριστοῦ ("**we have** peace with God through our Lord Jesus Christ"), others have the subjunctive, **ἔχωμεν**, which would read as a hortatory subjunctive ("**let us have** peace with God"). If this latter is the correct reading, Paul would be exhorting the Roman believers to reconcile with God on the basis of Christ's sacrificial death on the cross which brought justification to all who believe (see Rom 3:23–25).

Although the subjunctive (ἔχωμεν) has somewhat better textual support, most scholars consider the indicative (ἔχομεν) to be the original reading, since it fits Paul's theological argument in the letter much better. As Metzger says, "Since in this passage it appears that Paul is not exhorting but stating facts ('peace' is the possession of those who have been justified), only the indicative is consonant with the apostle's argument."[1]

---

1. B. M. Metzger, *A Textual Commentary on the Greek New Testament,* 2nd ed. (United Bible Societies, 2000), 452.

VERB

What It Looks Like

Verbs in Greek are built on verbal stems and then inflected with prefixes and suffixes to indicate tense, voice, mood, person, and number. Various components of a verb can be illustrated using the first aorist active indicative third person plural:

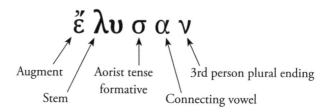

What It Does

Verbs are words that describe an action or a state of being. Greek verbs are inflected with reference to five features: *tense, voice, mood, person,* and *number*:

1. *Tense* can indicate two things: (1) *time* of action and (2) *aspect,* or *kind of* action. Aspect is primary. Only in the INDICATIVE mood does tense indicate time.[1]

   a. *Time.* Three kinds of time:
      - *Past.* Usually expressed with the AORIST ("I ate"), IMPERFECT ("I was eating"), PERFECT ("I have eaten"), or PLUPERFECT ("I had eaten") in the indicative mood.
      - *Present.* Usually expressed with the PRESENT tense ("I eat").
      - *Future.* Usually expressed with the FUTURE tense ("I will eat").

   b. *Aspect.* Three main kinds of action:
      - *Imperfective.* Focuses on the progress or process of the action. The tense forms are the PRESENT and IMPERFECT.
      - *Perfective.* Views the action in summary, from the outside as a whole. The tense form is the AORIST.
      - *Stative.* Describes a state of affairs or condition that exists. Tense forms are the PERFECT or PLUPERFECT.

---

1. Some grammarians reject the idea that tense has anything to do with time *in any mood*. See S. E. Porter, *Verbal Aspect in the Greek of the New Testament, with Reference to Tense and Mood*, 3rd ed., Studies in Biblical Greek (New York: Peter Lang, 1989), as well as the helpful summary and bibliography in C. R. Campbell, *Advances in the Study of Greek: New Insights for Reading the New Testament* (Grand Rapids: Zondervan, 2015), 105–33. For the view espoused here, see B. M. Fanning, *Verbal Aspect in New Testament Greek* (Oxford: Clarendon, 1991) and Wallace, *Grammar*, 504–12.

2. *Voice* indicates whether the subject is acting or being acted upon. Three voices:
   a. ACTIVE. The subject is acting: "He eats."
   b. PASSIVE. The subject is being acted upon: "He is eaten" (by a lion?).
   c. MIDDLE (not in English). The subject in some sense participates in the action: "He washes (himself)."

3. *Mood* indicates the relationship of the action to reality.
   a. INDICATIVE. Real action ("I eat").
   b. SUBJUNCTIVE. Potential action ("I may eat").
   c. IMPERATIVE. Commanded action ("Eat!").
   d. OPTATIVE. Mood of wishing ("May you be filled").

4. *Person* indicates who is participating in the action.
   a. 1ˢᵗ PERSON = The one who is speaking ("I," "we").
   b. 2ⁿᵈ PERSON = The one spoken to ("you").
   c. 3ʳᵈ PERSON = The one spoken about ("he," "she," "it," "they").

5. *Number* indicates the number of subjects, whether singular or plural.

An Exegetical Insight

Present tense verbs *in general* indicate continuous or progressive action. This is especially so outside the indicative mood. Knowing this may help to explain one of the more difficult passages in the New Testament. 1 John 3:6, 9 reads:

> πᾶς ὁ ἐν αὐτῷ μένων οὐχ **ἁμαρτάνει**· πᾶς **ὁ ἁμαρτάνων** οὐχ ἑώρακεν αὐτὸν οὐδὲ ἔγνωκεν αὐτόν. . . . Πᾶς ὁ γεγεννημένος ἐκ τοῦ θεοῦ **ἁμαρτίαν** οὐ **ποιεῖ**, ὅτι σπέρμα αὐτοῦ ἐν αὐτῷ μένει, καὶ οὐ **δύναται ἁμαρτάνειν**, ὅτι ἐκ τοῦ θεοῦ γεγέννηται.

> "No one who remains in him **sins**. No **one who sins** has seen him or knows him. . . . No one who is born of God **practices sin**, because his seed remains in him; and he **is** not **able to sin** because he is born of God."

These verses seem to suggest that true Christians will cease sinning, but this, of course, is *not* the experience of most Christians. Many commentators point out that the two verbs (ἁμαρτάνει; ποιεῖ), the participle (ἁμαρτάνων), and the infinitive (ἁμαρτάνειν) are all in the present tense, and are probably *customary presents*. If so, John would not be referring to individual sins, but to the fact that no one who perpetually practices a sinful lifestyle is born of God (cf. NIV).[2]

---

2. For a different view (that these are *gnomic presents*), see Wallace, *Grammar*, 524–25.

VOCATIVE

What It Looks Like

The vocative case is by far the rarest case in the New Testament. There are only 609 nouns in the vocative in the NT, and just five words make up over half of these occurrences. The following chart includes all the vocatives that occur ten times of more in the New Testament and compares the nominative form to the vocative. Notice that the key distinguishing mark of many vocative singulars is the epsilon (ε) ending. Others look the same as the nominative case. The vocative plurals are always the same as the nominative plurals. Because there are so few vocatives, it is best to become familiar with the most common words and forms rather than trying to memorize paradigm charts. You can usually recognize vocatives in context because they are set off from the sentence with commas: **κύριε**, τίς ἐπίστευσεν τῇ ἀκοῇ ἡμῶν; ("**Lord**, who has believed our message?"; Rom 10:16).

Vocative Nouns That Occur Ten Times or More in the New Testament

Nominative Singular	Vocative Singular	Voc./Nom. Plural	Translation	Frequency
κύριος	κύριε	κύριοι	lord/lords	124
ἀδελφός	ἀδελφέ	ἀδελφοί	brother(s); sibling(s)	112
πατήρ	πατέρ	πατέρες	father(s); ancestor(s)	35
ἀνήρ	ἄνερ	ἄνδρες	man/men	33
διδάσκαλος	διδάσκαλε	διδάσκαλοι	teacher(s)	31
γυνή	γύναι	γυναῖκες	woman/women; wife/wives	13
θεός	θεέ	θεοί	God/gods	13
ῥαββί	ῥαββί	–	Rabbi	13
τέκνον	τέκνον	τέκνα	child/children	12
ὑποκριτής	ὑποκριτά	ὑποκριταί	hypocrite(s)	12
βασιλεύς	βασιλεῦ	βασιλεῖς	king(s)	11
υἱός	υἱε	υἱοί	son(s); child(ren)	11
Ἰησοῦς	Ἰησοῦ	–	Jesus	10

What It Does

The vocative case is one of five Greek cases. The others are NOMINATIVE, GENITIVE, DATIVE, and ACCUSATIVE. The vocative is the case of direct address, when someone is addressed by a name, title, or descriptor. There is some debate as to whether the vocative should be considered a case at all, since case normally refers to the function of a word in a sentence, and the vocative is syntactically independent of the rest of the sentence. Yet, while independent within the sentence, the vocative does carry discourse meaning with reference to the rest of the sentence by identifying the person or thing being addressed.

There are two main kinds of address in the New Testament, *simple* and *emphatic*. Simple is the vocative alone. Emphatic is the vocative with the particle ὦ ("O").

- *Simple.*

  ἐξομολογοῦμαί σοι, **πάτερ**, **κύριε** τοῦ οὐρανοῦ καὶ τῆς γῆς.
  "I praise you, **Father**, **Lord** of heaven and earth." (Matt 11:25)

- *Emphatic.*

  ὦ γύναι, μεγάλη σου ἡ πίστις.
  "**O woman**, your faith is great." (Matt 15:28)

An Exegetical Insight

Translation always involves interpretation, since languages and cultures differ from one another. Translating the vocative illustrates well some of these challenges. Consider the vocative when Jesus addresses his mother in John 2:4:

λέγει αὐτῇ ὁ Ἰησοῦς· τί ἐμοὶ καὶ σοί, **γύναι**; οὔπω ἥκει ἡ ὥρα μου.
"Jesus said to her, 'Why do you involve me, **woman**? My hour has not yet come.'"

Although γυνή commonly means "woman" (or "wife"), it sounds rude in English for Jesus to address his own mother in this way. But what sounds rude in English did not in Greek. Some versions use other terms (NLT; NIV 1984; NCV: "dear woman"; CEV: "mother"); others provide explanatory footnotes. The NIV 2011 translates as "woman," but has a footnote reading, "The Greek for *Woman* does not denote any disrespect."

APPENDIX 1

The Greek Alphabet with Pronunciation

Upper Case[1]	Lower Case	Name	Transliteration	Pronunciation (Erasmian)
A	α	alpha	*a*	f<u>a</u>ther
B	β	beta	*b*	<u>b</u>ook
Γ	γ	gamma	*g*	<u>g</u>ot[3]
Δ	δ	delta	*d*	<u>d</u>og
E	ε	epsilon	*e*	s<u>e</u>t
Z	ζ	zeta	*z*	ga<u>z</u>e
H	η	eta	*ē*	th<u>ey</u>
Θ	θ	theta	*th*	<u>th</u>ing
I	ι	iota	*i*	<u>i</u>ntr<u>i</u>gue
K	κ	kappa	*k*	<u>k</u>ept
Λ	λ	lambda	*l*	<u>l</u>amb
M	μ	mu	*m*	<u>m</u>iddle
N	ν	nu	*n*	<u>n</u>ever
Ξ	ξ	xi	*x*	mi<u>x</u>
O	ο	omicron	*o*	<u>o</u>perate
Π	π	pi	*p*	<u>p</u>en
P	ρ	rho	*r*	<u>r</u>ight
Σ	σ, ς[2]	sigma	*s*	<u>s</u>imple
T	τ	tau	*t*	<u>t</u>able
Y	υ	upsilon	*u* or *y*	t<u>u</u>ne
Φ	φ	phi	*ph*	<u>ph</u>one
X	χ	chi	*ch*	lo<u>ch</u>
Ψ	ψ	psi	*ps*	lip<u>s</u>
Ω	ω	omega	*ō*	<u>o</u>nly

[1] Capital letters in Greek are used only (1) at the beginning of paragraphs, (2) at the beginning of direct quotes, and (3) with proper names.

[2] The "final sigma" (ς) is used when the sigma is the last letter in a word.

[3] The double gamma (γγ) is pronounced *ng*. ἄγγελος would be pronounced *angelos*.

APPENDIX 2

Diphthongs & Diaeresis

A *diphthong* is two vowels that make a single sound.

Diphthong	Pronunciation	Example
αι	<u>ai</u>sle	αἰτέω ("I ask")
ει	w<u>eig</u>ht	εἰς ("into")
οι	s<u>oi</u>l	οἶδα ("I know)
αυ	n<u>ow</u>	αὐλή ("courtyard")
ου	s<u>ou</u>p	οὐ ("not," "no")
υι	s<u>ui</u>te	υἱός ("son," "child")
ευ, ηυ	<u>eu</u>logy	εὐθύς ("immediately") ηὔξανεν ("he grew")

A *diaeresis* (ϊ) is two dots over a vowel used to indicate that the vowel is *not* part of a diphthong and that each vowel should be pronounced separately. It appears most commonly with foreign words in the New Testament, especially Hebrew names. The word Μωϋσῆς ("Moses"), for example, would be pronounced *mō-u-sās*.

APPENDIX 3

Accents, Breathing Marks, Punctuation

Accents

Greek accents indicate which syllable is stressed in pronunciation. There are three accents, which we demonstrate with the letter alpha (α).

Acute: ά
Grave: ὰ
Circumflex: ᾶ

In Classical Greek, accents indicated pitch or tone. The acute accent indicated a rising or high pitch; the grave accent a falling or low pitch; the circumflex pitch that both rose and fell on a single syllable. By the New Testament period the accents merely indicated a stressed syllable.

Rules related to accents are complex, but here are a few of the most basic:

1. An acute accent can appear on any of the last three syllables of a word.

2. A circumflex can occur on one of the last two syllables.

3. A grave accent can occur only on the last syllable and only if there is another word following it. If there is a punctuation mark following it or if it is listed as a vocabulary word, it will change to an acute accent.

4. If the last syllable has a long vowel, the accent must be on one of the last two syllables.

5. Nouns tend to keep the same accent location as their lexical form (the form you look up in the dictionary).

6. Verb accents tend to be recessive, which means they move as far toward the front of the word as the rules allow.

Breathing Marks

All words in Koine Greek that begin with a vowel or diphthong have a breathing mark, either a "rough" breathing mark ('), which is pronounced like an English *h*, or a "smooth" breathing mark ('), which is not pronounced.

Rough: ἁ
Smooth: ἀ

The Greek word ἐν ("in") has a smooth breathing mark and so would be pronounced *en*, while the Greek word ἕν ("one" [neuter]) has a rough breathing mark and so would be pronounced *hen*. For a diphthong, the breathing mark, like the accent, appears over the second vowel (e.g.: αἴρω, pronounced *īrō*; αἷμα, pronounced *hīma*). Words that begin with rho (ρ) also take a breathing mark.

Punctuation

Punctuation refers to marks and notations in a text that aid in understanding and correct reading, especially when reading aloud. While the Greeks used some kinds of punctuation as early as the fifth century BC, New Testament Greek manuscripts do not generally have punctuation (or spacing between words). The marks seen in a printed Greek New Testament are interpretive and were added by modern editors. There are four main punctuation marks in Greek:

1. The comma, a "half stop" or pause, is written the same as an English comma (,).

2. The period, a "full stop," is written the same as an English period (.).

3. The semicolon, a "three-quarter stop," which in English is written as a comma with a dot above it (;), is a raised dot in Greek (·).

4. The question mark (?) is written in Greek like a semicolon (;).

Punctuation	English	Greek
Comma	,	,
Period	.	.
Semicolon	;	·
Question mark	?	;

SCRIPTURE INDEX

Genesis
28:12 75

Exodus
20:13–17 33
21:24 77

Leviticus
11:44 . . . . .41, 69

Deuteronomy
5:17–21 33

Psalms
2:7 69
14:1 69

Isaiah
56:7 69

Matthew
2:16 13
3:1 20
3:4 20
3:17 81
4:4 69
5:2 39
5:4 67
5:6 67
5:45 13
5:46 84
6:5 27
6:13 24
6:19 11
6:25 29
6:31 95
6:33 58
8:13 81

8:23 . . . . .74, 92
9:18 63
10:31 37
11:11 44
11:21 44
11:25 99
12:31 35
12:46 73
14:3 13
15:23 67
15:27 51
15:28 . . . . .45, 99
17:22 67
19:16 15
19:18 33
20:28 77
21:3 82
21:13 69
22:29 63
22:37 33
23:2 24
23:31 29
24:18 20
24:27 35
25:12 69
26:56 17
26:65 44
27:2 20
27:13 20
27:5 49
27:42 90

Mark
1:1 53
1:5 66
1:12 79
2:5 79
2:7 . . . . .17, 41

2:10 41
4:37 27
6:50 37
8:33 37
9:1 82
9:31 32
9:33 39
9:37 65
9:40 89
9:43 15
10:44 58
10:45 77
11:30 25
14:44 . . . . .29, 73
15:2 40
16:2 59
16:6 37

Luke
1:10 17
1:21 74
1:32 . . . . .15, 81
2:41 39
3:15 61
3:22 13
4:8 92
4:9 41
4:34 . . . . .44, 45
5:15 92
5:30 92
6:19 74
6:20 39
7:27 44
7:36 82
7:36–49 23
7:39 23
7:41–43 23
8:2 83

BIBLE SOFTWARE

Premier Bible Software

Accordance Bible Software. (PC and Mac). Developed by OakTree Software, Inc. (www.accordancebible.com).

BibleWorks. (PC and Mac). Developed by BibleWorks LLC (www.bibleworks. com).

Logos Bible Software. (PC and Mac). Developed by Logos Research Systems, Inc. (www.logos.com).

Other Bible Software (online or downloadable)

Bible Gateway. (www.biblegateway.com)

BibleSoft. PC/Mac Study Bible (PC and Mac) (biblesoft.com). Basic sample program is free.

Blue Letter Bible. (www.blueletterbible.org)

E-Sword. (www.e-sword.net)

QuickVerse. (PC and Mac) (www.lifeway.com/Product/ quickverse-bible-suite-10-P005537619)

WORDSearch. (PC and Mac) (wordsearchbible.com). WORDSearch Basic is free.

SELECT BIBLIOGRAPHY FOR FURTHER STUDY

Beginning Greek Grammars

Black, David Alan. *Learn to Read New Testament Greek*. 3rd ed. Nashville: Broadman & Holman, 2009.

Decker, Rodney J. *Reading Koine Greek: An Introduction and Integrated Workbook*. Grand Rapids: Baker, 2014.

Mounce, William D. *Basics of Biblical Greek*. 3rd ed. Grand Rapid: Zondervan, 2009.

Porter, Stanley E., Jeffrey T. Reed, and Matthew Brook O'Donnell. *Fundamentals of New Testament Greek*. Grand Rapids: Eerdmans, 2010.

Basic Grammar Help

Lamerson, Samuel. *English Grammar to Ace New Testament Greek*. Grand Rapids: Zondervan, 2004.

Long, Gary A. *Grammatical Concepts 101 for Biblical Greek: Learning Biblical Greek Grammatical Concepts through English Grammar*. Peabody, MA: Hendrickson, 2006.

Mounce, William D. *Greek for the Rest of Us: The Essentials of Biblical Greek*. 2nd ed. Grand Rapid: Zondervan, 2013.

Intermediate Greek Grammars

Brooks, James A., and Carlton Winbery. *Syntax of New Testament Greek*. Lanham, MD: University Press of America, 1978.

Dana, H. E., and J. R. Mantey. *A Manual Grammar of the Greek New Testament*. Toronto: Macmillan, 1927.

Moule, C. F. D. *An Idiom Book of New Testament Greek*. 2nd ed. Cambridge: Cambridge University Press, 1959.

Porter, S. E. *Idioms of the Greek New Testament*. 2nd ed. Sheffield: JSOT, 1992.

Smyth, H. W. *Greek Grammar*. Revised by G. M. Messing. Cambridge, MA: Harvard University Press, 1956.

Wallace, Daniel B. *The Basics of New Testament Syntax: An Intermediate Greek Grammar*. Grand Rapids: Zondervan, 1996. (Abridgement of *Greek Grammar Beyond the Basics*; see below).

———. *Greek Grammar Beyond the Basics. An Exegetical Syntax of the New Testament*. Grand Rapids: Zondervan, 1996.

Young, R. A. *Intermediate New Testament Greek: A Linguistic and Exegetical Approach*. Nashville: Broadman, 1994.

Zerwick, M. *Biblical Greek: Illustrated by Examples*. Rome: Pontifical Biblical Institute, 1963.

Advanced Greek Grammars

Blass, F., and A. Debrunner. *A Greek Grammar of the New Testament and Other Early Christian Literature*. Translated and revised by R. W. Funk. Chicago: University of Chicago Press, 1961.

Moulton, J. H. *A Grammar of New Testament Greek*. 4 vols. Edinburgh: T&T Clark, 1908–76.

Robertson, A. T. *A Grammar of the Greek New Testament in the Light of Historical Research*. 4th ed. New York: Hodder & Stoughton, 1923.